NEVER MIND THE BOLLOCKS, HERE'S THE SEX PISTOLS

THE SEX PISTOLS

CLASSIC ROCK ALBUMS
Series Editor: Clinton Heylin

NEVER MIND THE BOLLOCKS, HERE'S THE SEX PISTOLS

THE SEX PISTOLS

Clinton Heylin

SCHIRMER BOOKS
An Imprint of Simon & Schuster Macmillan
New York

Prentice Hall International
London   Mexico City   New Delhi   Singapore   Sydney   Toronto

The author and publisher are grateful for permission to quote from the following:

Review of *Never Mind the Bollocks, Here's the Sex Pistols* by Kris Needs, from Zigzag, December 1977. Copyright © by Kris Needs. Used by permission.

Review of *Never Mind the Bollocks, Here's the Sex Pistols* by Julie Burchill, from New Musical Express, 5 November 1977. Copyright © by New Musical Express. Used by permission.

Review of *Never Mind the Bollocks, Here's the Sex Pistols* by Chris Brazier, from Melody Maker, 5 November 1977. Copyright © by Melody Maker. Used by permission.

Review of *Never Mind the Bollocks, Here's the Sex Pistols* by Paul Nelson, from Rolling Stone, March 1978. Copyright © by Straight Arrow Publishers, Inc. Used by permission.

Schirmer Books
An Imprint of Simon & Schuster Macmillan
1633 Broadway
New York, NY 10019

Library of Congress Catalog Card Number: 97–29050

Printed in the United States of America

Printing Number
10 9 8 7 6 5 4 3 2 1

Library of Congress Cataloging-in-Publication Data

Heylin, Clinton
    Never mind the bollocks, here's the Sex Pistols : The Sex Pistols / Clinton Heylin.
        p. cm. — (Classic rock albums)
        ISBN 0–02–864726–2 (alk. paper)
        1. Sex Pistols (Musical group). Never mind the bollocks, here's the Sex Pistols.
2. Punk rock music—History and criticism. I. Title. II. Series.
        ML421.S4H49 1998
782.42166'2—dc21   97–29050
[B]   CIP
                                                                                            MN

This paper meets the requirements of ANSI/NISO Z.39.48–1992 (Permanence of Paper).

CONTENTS

INTRODUCTION
1

THE EARLY REPERTOIRE
5

THE SPEDDING DEMOS
14

THE GOODMAN DEMOS
21

THE ROAD TO EMI
27

THE FIRST ANARCHY SESSIONS
33

THE MIKE THORNE SESSION
41

THE SECOND ANARCHY SESSIONS
44

NOTORIETY BECKONS
53

THE GOOSEBERRY SESSIONS
57

GOD SAVE THE QUEEN, VACANT, AND A&M
63

THE PRICE IS PAID
72

THE PISTOLS ON VIRGIN
79

GOD SAVE SEX PISTOLS
87

BOLLOCKS: THE FINAL SEQUENCE
92

SPUNK AND THE ART OF CHAOS
101

THE RECEPTION AWAITING BOLLOCKS
105

BOLLOCKS ON TRIAL
109

THE REPUTE OF BOLLOCKS
118

THE SONGS
121

THE REVIEWS
139

DISCOGRAPHY
153

INDEXES
161

CONTENTS

INTRODUCTION

"IF PEOPLE BOUGHT THE RECORDS
FOR THE MUSIC, THIS THING WOULD HAVE DIED A DEATH LONG
AGO."

—**Malcolm McLaren,** *(London)*
Sunday Times, **November 19, 1977.**

The Sex Pistols' career was brief, spanning a mere twenty-six months and less than one hundred gigs, but the process by which they contained their sound in the studio has remained a maze in need of a little unwinding. Commencing with their first demo session—at Majestic Studios in May 1976—their time in the studio concluded fifteen months later with the recording of the final track for their solitary official album, *Never Mind the Bollocks,* the rant-driven "Bodies." In that time, they recorded just fifteen tracks from their own pens for possible release. These fifteen self-penned tracks (plus half a dozen covers, recorded at Wessex, between multiple attempts at "Anarchy in the UK," and released posthumously on *The Great Rock & Roll Swindle*) comprise the most succinct ouevre of any premier division rock and roll band.

All but two of the originals on *Bollocks* came from the era when the Pistols were a living, breathing, gigging entity, on the boards weekly, and blessed with an incumbent bassist, Glen Matlock, who could dunk a tune into the band's bucketful of brawn. (It amazes me the number of people who have queried how The Sex Pistols could re-form in 1996 without Sid

Vicious!) Matlock was fired from the band in February 1977, going on to form his own powerpoppers, The Rich Kids. The residue trio, with novice junkie John Beverly aka Sid Vicious taking up bass duties (though not in the studio, and only after some lessons from Matlock), mustered just three more ditties in the eleven months it took before Vicious test-ran an overdose, Rotten took a New York raincheck, and Jones and Cook insisted on flying down to Rio.

Yet recording these fifteen songs proved to be no simple matter. The boys worked their way through five producers in the search for the quintessential Pistols sound—or, more to the point, an accurate reflection of that sound, audible at any Pistols show in 1976. The Pistols rejected Chris Spedding of "Motorbiking" fame as a possible producer, although it was Spedding who was responsible for their first foray into the studio, three demos one afternoon in May 1976. The man responsible for convincing his superiors at EMI to sign these misfits, Mike Thorne, also only fleetingly satisfied an ambition to produce the Pistols, spending a single afternoon in EMI's eight-track demo studio in Manchester Square shortly before the Pistols were unceremoniously dropped by the label. The two studio hands who would complete *Never Mind the Bollocks*—Chris Thomas and Bill Price—were brought in only after EMI (their original record label) was dissatisfied with the results the foursome achieved with Dave Goodman, the band's first choice and manager McLaren's continuing choice, though after the Pistols were hoofed off EMI, McLaren paid for a week of sessions at Gooseberry in January 1977 with Goodman again producing.

But it was Chris Thomas—sometime producer of The Beatles, Roxy Music, and the reviled Pink Floyd—and Wessex Whizkid engineer Bill Price who finally provided the technical tweezers that prised out "Anarchy in the UK" and, in a single session four months later, contrived to provide its two sibling 45s—"God Save the Queen" and "Pretty Vacant"—in rock's most explosive triple-whammy.

Dave Goodman ended up with just two bona fide credits on those singles, the B-sides "I Wanna Be Me" and "No Fun" (another Goodman demo, "No Feelings," was to have been the original B-side of the aborted "God Save The Queen" 45 planned for release by A&M). It is almost as if the factions within the band (or Glitterbest, the management company formed by McLaren) could never determine which sound suited them

best, the rough-and-ready recordings made with Goodman or the supra-pro, multilayered results Thomas (and Price) produced. Or perhaps the Pistols sought to be all things to all punks, the Small Faces *and* Slik.

Even though Goodman's work does not constitute any part of the finished *Bollocks,* a Goodman/Pistols album was always available. A genuine alternative to *Bollocks,* the legendary bootleg LP *Spunk* snuck its nose in the air barely a week before the "authorized" version. If The Beatles' original, pre-Spector version of *Let it Be—Get Back, and Twelve Other Songs*—was, in Lennon's words, "what it was [really] like," so was Goodman's album. In fact, Goodman can claim the greatest experience of the boys in the studio. He also came closest to "how they really sounded" (to his ears) with the famous Denmark Street demos of July 1976 and his original, Wessex "Anarchy"—the one originally intended to be "vinyl quotation number one." In three separate week-long bouts with the Pistols over a six-month period, sampling their sound on four-, eight-, sixteen-, and twenty-four-track, Goodman recorded all but one of the thirteen self-penned originals that date from the Matlock era (everything save "Did You No Wrong"). These twelve tracks, in their Denmark Street, Wessex, and Gooseberry guises, comprise *Spunk*—the alternate *Bollocks.*

In 1996, twenty years after the Pistols were at their mountaintop-peak, Virgin UK finally gave fans *Bollocks* and *Spunk* in a single jewel box, marketed on the back of the Return of these Revenants. A twofer CD set—called *This Is Crap* on the tray but *Bollocks/Spunk* on the spine—gave the world a newly remastered *Never Mind the Bollocks* (though not the two Thomas-Price B-sides, "Did You No Wrong" and "Satellite," found on *Kiss This,* a previous single-CD repackaging of *Bollocks*). It also incorporated the twelve-track version of *Spunk,* all three May 1976 Spedding demos (in pin-drop quality, finally dispelling oft-voiced myths about competency and credits), and five previously unbootlegged *Bollocks* alternate takes. Even though the *Spunk* tracks are a notch down in sound quality from earlier CD versions (i.e., Goodman's *The Mini Album* and the DoJo offering *Early Daze,* which also affords listeners the opportunity to hear the songs in the correct chronological order), this Virgin double-header is likely to remain the ultimate Pistols studio set for some time to come (that is, until Virgin gives us the full Wessex Goodman tapes—including those that found their way onto the semi-kosher *Pirates of Destiny* CD—plus the full, unedited seven-minute "No Fun"; the Mike Thorne session; the remaining *Bollocks* demos [there may be more]; those two Thomas-Price B-sides; and, even—hang the expense—the original four-track roughs of the Denmark Street tapes, three of which can be found on one of the many Goodman hodgepodge releases: *Wanted: The Goodman Tapes*).

We now have the almost unique opportunity to hear a classic rock repertoire in two distinct studio guises: the Jonesian universe of guitar-soup versus the live-means-alive approach of novice producer Dave Goodman, ever encouraged by the Pistols' novice Svengali, Malcolm McLaren. Readers may surmise that the contradictions that abound in their studio recordings are the very ones that curtailed their existence, making the story of *Bollocks* somewhat resemble that of the rise and fall of The Sex Pistols.

THE EARLY REPERTOIRE

Chronology is important. The pace with which the Pistols were adopted as banner-carriers by a select few Kritics, ex-hippy entrepreneurs, and bored pub-rockers certainly suggests that cometh the hour, cometh the band. The Pistols, who made their live debut on November 6, 1975, were reviewed by *NME* editor-in-waiting Neil Spencer playing support to Southend pub-rock rowdies Eddie & the Hot Rods at the Marquee in February 1976; occupied a full two-page spread in *NME*'s main rival, *Sounds,* in April 1976; and recorded their first demos with noted guitarist/producer Chris Spedding the following month, barely six months after their St. Martin's College of Art debut. In the interim they had also been banned from the Marquee and the Nashville, the two key London outlets for any such band of upstarts, as a result of in-house fracases instigated by the band and/or its motley retinue, the notorious Bromley Contingent.

The speed with which the Pistols came to the attention of a (national) music press should perhaps be contrasted with the ennervating New York punk scene which was allowed to gestate for nearly eighteen months—between the spring of 1974 and the fall of 1975—before a handful of self-appointed scenester-critics grew tired of the silence and finally wrote each other up. Like Television before them, when the Pistols got their first review, just three months after their live debut, there were no partners-in-crime, no scene, no fun.

From day one, it seems the Pistols were at the epicenter of an argument in ever decreasing circles. Even before they made their first demos, they had generated a fair few column inches in the UK music press vis-

Don't look over your shoulder, but the Sex Pistols are coming

Sex Pistols
MARQUEE

"HURRY UP, they're having an orgy on stage," said the bloke on the door as he tore the tickets up.

I waded to the front and staightway sighted a chair arcing gracefully through the air, skidding across the stage and thudding contentedly into the PA system, to the obvious nonchalance of the bass drums and guitar.

Well I didn't think they sounded *that* bad on first earful — then I saw it was the singer wh'd done the throwing.

He was stalking round the front rows, apparently scuffing over the litter on the floor between baring his teeth at the audience and stopping to chat to members of the group's retinue. He's called Johnny Rotten and the monicker fits.

Sex Pistols? Seems I'd missed the cavortings with the two scantily clad (plastic thigh boots and bodices) pieces dancing up front. In fact, I only caught the last few numbers; enough, as it happens, to get the idea. Which is . . . a quarter of spiky teenage misfits from the wrong end of various London roads, playing 60's styled white punk rock as unself-consciously as it's possible to play it these days i.e. self-consciously.

Punks? Springsteen Bruce and the rest of 'em would get shredded if they went up against these boys. They've played less than a dozen gigs as yet, have a small but fanatic following, and don't get asked back. Next month they play the Institute of Contemporary Arts if that's a clue.

I'm told the Pistols repertoire includes lesser known Dave Berry and Small Faces numbers (check out early Kinks' B sides leads), besides an Iggy and the Stooges item and several self-penned numbers like the moronic "I'm Pretty Vacant', a meandering power-chord job that produced the chair-throwing incident.

No-one asked for an encore but they did one anyway: "We're going to play 'Substitute'."

"You can't play," heckled an irate French punter.

"So what?" countered the bassman, jutting his chin in the direction of the bewildered Frog.

That's how it is with the Pistols — a musical experience with the emphasis on Experience.

"Actually, we're not into music," one of the Pistols confided afterwards.

Wot then?

"We're into chaos."

Neil Spencer

Pistols' Johnny Rotten: it fits.

à-vis the question of (their) "musical chops" (and whether such "chops" need be de rigeur). The band even had the plug pulled on them just three songs into their first show—neatly parallelling the Velvet Underground's debut ten years earlier.

It may seem a tad peculiar when viewed from an aural landscape bequeathed by the Pistols to the likes of Nirvana and Oasis, but circa 1976 music critics had a shall-we-say-tendency to consider a band's technical ability the be-all and end-all. In a sound born of the bastard son of the twelve-bar blues, not the glorious Ninth, playing the "right" notes had replaced rhythm and feel. *NME* had just voted *Sergeant Pepper's Lonely Hearts Club Band* the joint-greatest album in the edifice of Rock. (We can be but grateful it was alongside *Blonde on Blonde.*) The charts were chockful of pap: Expertly produced, all impurities homogenized, but pap nonetheless. The UK number-one singles that year included "Mamma

Mia," "Fernando," and "Dancing Queen" by Abba; "Forever and Ever" by Silk; "December 1963 (Oh, What a Night)" by The Four Seasons; and "A Child Is Born" by Johnny Mathis, to name just a few choice picks.

Away from the preteen purchasers of this bevy of pop-schlock, 1976 was the era of ProgRock and concept albums of side-length songs. If Pink Floyd's *Wish You Were Here* was little more than variations on the Theme of Crazy Sid, Peter Gabriel's Genesis took the precepts of Jung the Foreman to new heights with their one-hundred-minute epic *The Lamb Lies Down on Broadway,* transplanted from stage to stage around the world through the winter and spring of 1974–1975. Even more primed for indulgence were Yes and Emerson, Lake and Palmer, both of whom insisted that three-album sets were required to truly represent their gratuitously self-important live performances. Hence the great divide: Album Bands and Single Bands. Time to tear down the walls.

Melody Maker, whose all-too-transparent ProgRock bias endured even through the house of punk, were (perhaps inevitably) the first national music paper to get on the Pistols' case. Reviewing the band's first show at the Nashville on April 3, the anonymous *MM* reviewer seemed more than a mite bemused:

> The whole contrived and misguided aesthetic of "they're so bad they're great" has, with the Sex Pistols—a recently much-vaunted four-piece band of total incompetents from West London—been taken to unprecedented levels. Their dreadfully inept attempts to zero in on the kind of viciously blank intensity previously epitomised by The Stooges was rather endearing at first: the predictably moronic vocalist ("go on—pick yer nose," a fan encouraged him at one point) was cheerfully idiotic, and the lead guitarist, another surrogate punk suffering from a surfeit of Sterling Morrison, played with a determined disregard for taste or intelligence. The novelty of this retarded spectacle was, however, soon erased by their tiresome repetition of punk cliches. They do as much for music as World War Two did for the cause of peace. I hope we shall hear no more of them.

Melody Maker journos were not the only ones applying Rayban-quality critical blinkers. The *New Musical Express* may have sent their best man to the Marquee in February but, come May, they seem to have become decidedly short staffed. The final sentence of a review of the Pistols at the 100 Club in the weekly's May 31 issue stands as one of the great faux pas of Rockspeak: "It will take a far better band than [The Sex Pistols] to create a raw music for their generation."

As it happens, there is a tape of the Nashville show that the *MM* scribe found so offensive. The set that night comprised eight originals, "Did You No Wrong," "Seventeen," "No Feelings," "New York," "Submission," "Problems," "Satellite," and "Pretty Vacant," plus covers of Dave Berry's "No Lip," The Monkees' "Steppin' Stone," The Who's "Substitute," and The Stooges' "No Fun."

For a band that had made its live debut less than five months earlier, the Pistols sound as tight as your stereotypical Scot, save for a particularly disastrous "Pretty Vacant" which, in an attempt at slickness, segues out of a suitably manic "Satellite" (Rotten intoning over the song's jam out, "it must be love, true love, real love") but collapses midway through, just as Glen shouts, "Leave it out, we got one more number yet." Cook then beats out time until the rest of the band can jump back on board and Rotten, ever revelling in chaos, switches to "blah blah blah" mode, drawling, "Rock & roll, ahh rock & roll, the way it should be . . . we're so pretty." Adopting a more bellicose form, Rotten demands the audience should, "wake up, fuckers," determined to ride the waves of Eros until one and all land in a heap.

The Pistols' debut at the Nashville represented something of a turning point, hard-of-hearing journalists notwithstanding. Playing support to the 101ers, a band of teddy-boy pub-rockers that featured one Joe Strummer on lead vocals, the boys had been limping along on cheap, hired PAs and the trashed equipment of other wannabes. If not trashed at the evening's outset, the equipment was invariably garbage-can fodder by set end—hence their running feud with Eddie & the Hot Rods, whose monitors Rotten had unceremoniously kicked in at the Marquee two months earlier.) The Nashville required those extra volts, and McLaren was required to do a deal.

> DAVE GOODMAN: *I hired a PA to them when they played at the Nashville supporting the 101ers. We did it real cheap for the Albion Agency, and we felt we were conned into doing a cheap PA for the*

support band [because] the 101ers got full use of it [as well].
Indeed Strummer kicked in one of the monitors after he sat there
gobsmacked watching the Pistols. . . . Anyway, after the gig I said
to the band, "You got any more gigs? We like what you're doing."
"What???" "Yeah, man. It's like, back in '64 we had a band who
used to do all the Small Faces, some of the same songs,
'Substitute,' 'Whatcha Gonna Do About It,' and all that." They
seemed so young. And Malcolm was like, "Fucking hell, some-
one's offering us some help."

Also in attendance that night at the Nashville was another soul keen
to represent the Pistols as the sonic vanguard of his generation. Jonh
Ingham was a friendly journalist, and one of influence, who wrote up the
Pistols' debut at a Soho strip club the night after the Nashville. (It ran in
Sounds the same week as *Melody Maker*'s write-off.) Ingham came well
versed in an altogether more outre aesthetic, dismissing the
"Technicalists" with curt disdain:

If you hate Patti Smith for all that noise and rock & roll energy at
the expense of technique and sounding pretty, then you'll really
hate The Sex Pistols. Their aesthetic is Shepherd's Bush Who and
speed era Small Faces—they play it fast and they play it loud. The
guitarist doesn't bother too much with solos, just powering his way
through whatever passes as a middle eight. But this isn't to say
they're sloppy, far from it.

If the band's notoriety was always a mixed blessing, its first exposure to the studio came about as a direct result of the reputation it had
rapidly acquired for inept cacophony and direct confrontation. Among
the few who could tell the difference between in-your-face, gut-tugging
rock and sheer ineptitude was Chris Spedding, a well-known guitarist
who had himself jumped from sessionwork to notoriety in one three-
minute movement (i.e., "Motorbiking," a top 20 hit in September 1975).
Spedding was a regular at Malcolm McLaren and Vivienne Westwood's
King's Road shop, Sex, and had been since its Let It Rock days back in
1974 (when McLaren convinced himself the Teddy Boy revival was
about to sweep the nation). Spedding was first dragged along by a part-

time assistant at Sex, a Cleveland girl who carried her own retractable shoulder-chip.

> CHRIS SPEDDING: *I saw them at the 100 Club the first time they were there. Chrissie Hynde took me. I thought they were great. There was hardly anybody there. They'd frighten audiences away in those days. There'd be twenty people in the club at the beginning and about two by the time they finished playing. They used to have fights on stage and Rotten [would be constantly] running off stage. They were definitely what the business needed and I couldn't understand why people in the same business as me couldn't see it.*

The period Spedding is describing had largely come to an end by the time they played their first headlining gig at the 100 Club, on May 11, 1976. The Bromley Contingent, kids from a Kent "suburbia dream" who had now adopted the Pistols as the one band that spoke their lingo, were now regulars at all the London shows.

> CHRIS SPEDDING: *I offered to record them because . . . when they started getting some notoriety and nobody had really heard them, this was before they got into the musical press, I would meet people from the London musical press in clubs. And they knew that Malcolm McLaren and Vivienne Westwood were making my clothes, and they [would say], "Are you also getting involved with that terrible group that they've got, The Sex Pistols?" And I was like, "Well, everybody to their own opinion but where did you hear them?" "Oh, we haven't heard them but we know they're terrible." So I thought this was a classic injustice which could be easily rectified if they got taken into the studio so that people could hear them [properly].*

Most likely, Spedding first witnessed The Sex Pistols at their unbilled 100 Club debut on March 30, when they served as support act to one of the ubiquitous godawful pubrock combos searching for the Feelgood factor on the mid-1970s London pub circuit. (*Stupidity,* Dr. Feelgood's live album, had reached number one the previous summer, despite the absence of hit singles or media hype.) Spedding was not the only eyewitness that night at the 100 Club to recognize their potential. After the gig, clubowner Ron Watts offered the Pistols their own weekly residency in May on a traditionally "dead" night (Tuesday), commencing four days before they were to go in the studio with Spedding.

Spedding, though, was not about to go in the studio with such rookies without a little advance planning—like deciding what songs they should record.

> CHRIS SPEDDING: *I decided on the songs. I knew enough about this [that] I didn't want to go in and just have total anarchy. I knew enough about presenting something to record companies to know that they wanted three songs usually. So I went to a couple of rehearsals at their place in Denmark Street and got them to go through their whole repertoire and I took notes, and I chose . . . the three best songs that I thought they had at the time.*

Speddding was only interested in hearing the band's own songs. Of the eight originals featured in their live set in May 1976 (six of which were to comprise the core of *Never Mind the Bollocks*), at least four had been constituents of their earliest live shows. "Did You No Wrong," "Pretty Vacant," "Submission," and "Seventeen (Lazy Sod)" all appear on a pre-debut list of songs rehearsed. (See Lee Wood's *The Sex Pistols Day by Day* for a full listing.)

"Did You No Wrong" had in fact been the quartet's first original composition, when, sans Rotten, they were still set on calling themselves the Swankers. The tunesmith responsible for its lurching riff, one Wally Nightingale, the Swankers' original frontman and guitarist, would not receive due credit (or even a cut of the royalties) until a matter of months before his mysterious death in 1996. The original lyrics, apparently the work of Paul Cook, were radically overhauled upon Rotten's admission to the band. Their new frontman retained just the chorus and three lines of the opening verse.

The juvenile, original last line, "But in return I get treated so cruel," got quickly red-crayoned and replaced by the vastly superior "Why should I do it? Our love is untrue." Rotten's compact lyrical flair was a most unexpected bonus from the green-haired youth with the ripped T-shirt whom

McLaren had recruited as a frontman solely because of his beligerent stare. In Rotten's hands the chorus ("I did you no wrong / going outta my head") became an all-embracing denial of personal responsibility of the fuck-off-and-die variety.

At the time of their first demo session, "Did You No Wrong" was still the Pistols' regular opener, though soon to be superseded in turn by three new songs: "Flowers of Romance," which was actually a "joke" instrumental at the expense of "Can't Play" journos; "I Wanna Be Me"; and finally "Anarchy in the UK." It also gave Matlock and Jones a new career opportunity, nightly auditions for the Atonal Brothers, wailing off-key "outta my head" at seemingly random points. Sadly "Did You No Wrong" was destined to remain unrecorded by Matlock & Co., though in many ways it defined the Pistols' debt to a sixties Britpop sensibility.

If "Submission," "Seventeen," and "Pretty Vacant" were also part of the Pistols' early rehearsals, they appear on the first known live recording of the band, made at Welwyn Garden City on February 21, 1976 (a "St. Albans tape" purportedly from the February 19 is almost certainly incorrectly dated). The sole addition to these four originals at the February shows was a scathing riposte to the New York Dolls and their jaded, but oh-so-studied, decadence, "New York," aka "Looking for a Kiss," which was as much a sideswipe at their manager's abiding obsession with the Dolls as an attack on the Dolls themselves.

The three "home county" shows in mid-February—St. Albans, High Wycombe, and Welwyn Garden City—that coincided with their first press review was a way of keeping their hand in while their inexperienced and somewhat fey manager attempted to secure London gigs, a problem given: (1) his reluctance to play the London pub circuit and (2) the recently instituted ban at the Marquee, indicative of the band's fast-spreading notoriety. The six-week layoff that followed these shows evidently pushed the band into writing more songs, at least one of which was in part inspired by the band's rude introduction to life in the outer nebular of Commuterland, "Satellite": "I bet you're all so happy in suburbia dream / But I'm only laughing, You ain't in my scheme."

"Problems" and "No Feelings" also seemed borne of the frustrations that stemmed from a lack of acceptance, their due for some time to come. The impotent rage in a song like "Problems" ("The problem is you / whatcha gonna do?") is resolved in "No Feelings," but only by an act of irrational violence: "I kick you in the face/ You got nothing to say / I kick you in the head/ When you get down and pray."

Spedding presumably responded to the threat-made-explicit when he chose these two ditties, along with that riff of riffs "Pretty Vacant," to record at Majestic Studios, where he had arranged to convene with Cook, Jones, Matlock, and Rotten one Friday morning in May.

THE SPEDDING DEMOS

CHRIS SPEDDING: *I'd used the studio when I did the* Here Come the Warm Jets *album with Eno. And we got the same engineer, Derek Chandler. I got them to go in there ten o'clock in the morning, I got there about quarter to eleven, they were all set up, we started recording about eleven, about one o'clock we finished and I mixed them. I was out of there by four or five o'clock. There was two guitar overdubs, that was about it. I faded ["Pretty Vacant"] in, I thought that'd be a cute idea. . . . I said I'd bring my bass amp and my guitar amp. That's about the nearest I got to playing with them. They'd not been in the studio before. Sometimes an amp has a funny buzz and it doesn't record properly and they wouldn't know that unless they'd been in the studio. You get a little bit nervous if things don't go well the first time you get in the studio. [When] you hear your first tape back and it sounds horrible, all your confidence goes. I had my amps and I stood over the drums while he tuned the drums to get out all the buzzes. Fortunately his drums sounded pretty good anyway, so there was hardly anything for me to do, and I made sure that they had a headphone balance and that the singer in his isolation booth could hear all the instruments properly and I asked them to do a rehearsal for me and I switched on the recorder. So they thought they were doing a rehearsal and they were actually doing their first take. . . . I never really got them to hear themselves back and get all nervous about it until [they'd] more or less [finished]. "Next one, next song, try another song," and they were more or less first takes, first time in the studio. Later on with Dave Goodman they spent weeks and weeks wasting time*

Spedding's finger on Sex Pistols' trigger

THE SEX PISTOLS sneaked into Majestic Recording Studios recently with Chris Spedding (that's him second from right trying to out-punk the rest of the lads) as producer and managed to lay down three tracks, all of which were self written. Their precise future has not yet been determined but it is likely that at least one of them will find its way into your local record store in some form or other. ᴢ⍥·Ƽ·ᵼᏏ

and tape trying to get a representation of what Dave Goodman thought he heard live. I think his comment when he heard my tapes was that they sound dead. Knowing Dave Goodman's sound what he means is they have no echo. . . . Rotten sung live, but it was in an isolation booth so they could easily take them out. . . . You can actually hear the way the band played together, it's not like guitar-overdub soup, which was what happened on some of the [songs on Bollocks*].*

It seems to be a given that no producer ever admits that someone else got better results with a particular artist than they managed themselves. This certainly seems to be the case with the Pistols. Goodman, Spedding, and

Chris Thomas all seem convinced that they captured the Pistols' sound best. After Goodman heard Spedding's tape, he felt that the band sounded lost in as big a studio as Majestic. Thomas's take on the Spedding demos was equally dismissive: "I remember hearing the Spedding demos and not liking them, sorry Chris, 'cause it was like a RAK drum sound. . . . It reminded me of Suzie Quatro."

The belated release of the Majestic demos on *This Is Crap* suggests that, for an afternoon's work with a bunch of novices at an imposing studio like Majestic, Spedding certainly harnessed something, if not entirely capturing the sense of violence that was then bound up with the Pistols' whole sound (which became dissipated as the visual threat grew). When Steve Jones called the Spedding demos "more poppy," one suspects he was voicing a personal dissatisfaction with how he came across. Although Thomas is right to decry the drum sound, which thuds without remit, the songs pile along well enough. The guitarist in Spedding, however, could not resist the conventionalities of guitarspeak and so, on "Problems," as a guitar solo absent from live performances is introduced, the guitar suddenly zooms up in the mix. On "No Feelings," the song's main riff reappears as some kind of leitmotif every now and then, dubbed atop the simple chugging rhythm of the basic track.

The May 1976 "Pretty Vacant," as Spedding indicates, fades both in and out. The fade-out is particularly effective as Jones plays that moronic riff in such a way that it sounds like an infinite number of monkeys have abandoned their random search for Beethoven's Fifth and have come up with this simple two-note thing that they are determined to keep playing until the crack of doom. However, the intro comes across as plain lame, displaying that "determined disregard for taste or intelligence" that may have been the composer Matlock's intention—"the Blank Generation idea was linked to discussions we'd be having around the band . . . so what I was trying to do was take those kind of ideas and make them really simple"—but would not have had A&R guys leaping tall buildings to beat a path to their door. "Pretty Vacant" needed beefing up, even if Glen's mum was impressed.

GLEN MATLOCK: *We did the demo session at Majestic Studios, a cinema converted into a twenty-four-track studio just off Clapham High Road near the common. I used Spedding's amp as my bass amp and that was the closest he came to playing with the Pistols while I was around. As always in the studio, things went slower than expected and the time went so quickly that we ran out of money before we got round to mixing what we'd recorded, which was three songs. . . . When I got home to Greenford . . . my mum said, "Where have you been all day?" I told her I'd been recording in the studio and suddenly she got all interested and asked to hear what I'd done. So I played her the unmixed tape I'd brought home with me. "Oooo," she said, "I like the first one, it sounds just like The Shadows." That was "Pretty Vacant."*

What Spedding did manage to capture was a sense of the bellicose energy that was Rotten the Frontman. Like all the best Pistols recordings, there is a hoarseness that gives Rotten's voice a razor edge, suggestive of a man tired of shouting the truth, locked in to an intensity that suggests this is one singer playing for keeps.

Perhaps inevitably, the demos failed to convince detractors that here was a band with good hooks, a menacing vocalist, and a pile driver for a rhythm section. Adding insult to injury, a whispering campaign began suggesting that those ringing guitar overdubs, absent from the band's live sound, were being played by Spedding himself.

CHRIS SPEDDING: *As soon as they got on record, everyone thought it was me playing the guitar . . . [but] it's all [Jones]. Just imagine me championing a group when their guitar player was so bad that I had to do their parts for them. I would never have done it.*

The Spedding demos may have passed straight into lore, but they did generate a news feature in *Sounds,* courtesy of Jonh Ingham, with a photo of the boys and Spedding at Majestic and the headline, "Spedding's finger on Sex Pistols' trigger." Ingham suggested, somewhat optimistically, that "it is likely that at least one of [the demos] will find its way into your local record store in some form or other." However, there is no evidence that McLaren ever had any intention of achieving world domination by such a roundabout route as issuing an independent single. This, after all, was pre-Stiff, and the notion of an independent single as a way of attracting the attention of the "Majors" was a technique yet to make its way across the Atlantic. (Patti Smith's independently released "Piss Factory," Television's "Little Johnny Jewel," and Pere Ubu's "Heart of Darkness" had already established the notion stateside.)

According to Matlock, the demos also found their way into the hands of RAK head honcho Mickie Most—hardly surprising considering that Majestic was a RAK studio, and Spedding and Most were old cohorts.

> GLEN MATLOCK: *Subsequently, I found out that Mickie Most—who owned the RAK label, which Spedding was on—was interested in the band. Malcolm [had] made out that he was paying for those demos and that he would take the cost out of any gig money we made.*

> CHRIS SPEDDING: *I played the tape to somebody at RAK records and their A&R guy went to [EMI A&R man] Nick Mobbs, 'cause RAK was distributed by EMI, and said, "Look what Chris Spedding's come up with." Mobbs said, "I wouldn't touch them with a ten-foot pole. They're terrible."*

In his review of the first El Paradiso gig, back in April, Jonh Ingham bemoaned the fact that "unfortunately, you couldn't hear any lyrics . . . which annoyed the singer just as much. In the second song, he rammed the mike stand back and the cymbals went over. At the end of the third he berated the audience: 'Clap, you fuckers, because I'm wasting my time not hearing myself.'" The unfortunate *NME* reviewer at the first May 100 Club show also complained, "The [covers] were the only . . . songs I recognized through the wall of sound."

By the beginning of June, however, the Pistols had successfully slipped their lead and were unleashing performances that shared a searing intensity. Their first foray to the second home of the punk revolution, Manchester, took place in front of seventy wayward souls and at least two tape recorders. A cassette recording of the concert that lit the torch for Howard Devoto and Pete Shelley to form Buzzcocks, Steven Morrissey to pen curious letters to the music papers, and members of Joy Division to work on a first blueprint, bespoke—in Jon Savage's words—"a quantum leap from the Nashville [shows] in April." At the Manchester show an

aspirant writer by the name of Paul Morley found his first "punk" experience inspiring some of his best lines:

> The rough, raw tidal surge transforms the quartet into one neat unit
> of aloof intimidating punks. Guitar, bass, adopt suitable respectable
> easy-split stances. Rotten plays Frankenstein playing Lionel Blair
> with a hint of the forced mechanism of Bowie, Ferry and Bygraves.
> Technically they're accomplished. Defined limits, but they're disci-
> plined and don't stray. Hard, loud, clean, brisk and as relentless
> and guiltless as a zipless fuck. Their harmonies are spot off. If one
> of their songs ventures past the 200 second mark, they content-
> edly sustain the nifty moronic monotonous peak they initially
> attained. They plagiarise admirably . . . The Pistols' own songs are
> London mirror takes of verlaines New York violent rejections and
> sexual rebuttals. They're excellent.

This was the band that needed to be caught on tape, and not from the
echoey back wall of an upstairs room at the Free Trade Hall. Nor, indeed,
the oblong crypt that was the 100 Club, where the Pistols, having established one residency, returned in mid-June, and where another taper captured them at month's end, pushing themselves through another fifteen-
song set. The 100 Club was fast becoming almost a weekly refuge. The
London equivalent of New York's CBGBs, it welcomed what others
spurned, and cultivated what others let die. (On July 6 the support act was
The Damned.) If the seventy Manchester converts had whooped and
cajoled two encores out of the band, such acceptance was rare: save at
the 100 Club. On June 29 the Pistols unveiled two retorts to the gutter-
snipes of a national music press. one a caterwaul of inarticulacy, "Flowers
of Romance," and the other Rotten's most barbed use of English to date,
"I Wanna Be Me": "Down in the dark, down in the crypt / Down in the dark
where the typewriter fits / You wanna be someone / You wanna be me."

The 100 Club was where such tryouts could take place. As Jon
Savage observes in his grandiloquent text on punk origins, *England's
Dreaming:*

> In the intimate setting of the 100 Club, the group could relax
> enough to take risks with their material and their performances.

There they began to master their environment, using the acoustics of the small club to experiment with overload, feedback and distortion. Electric amplification had provided much of the excitement of early Rock & Roll: pushing their equipment to the limit—even further than the early Who—The Sex Pistols twisted their limited repertoire into a noise as futuristic as their rhetoric.

THE GOODMAN DEMOS

Soundman Dave Goodman had begun to shape the Pistols' sound live, adding a few effects and, above all, getting that important mix, LOUD but Audible (Grunge rockers: take note!). He was also itching to produce the band. If McLaren had entertained hopes of convincing labels of the hot property in their midst, the Spedding demos were not about to fulfill them. A single day in a twenty-four track studio was never likely to recarve Rock, maaaan. On the other hand, McLaren could hardly afford to invest the sums required to clock up serious studio time in the hope of catching the true flavor of the new sound, one that became the Pistols. The intimidating atmosphere of a cavernous studio like Majestic might just get in the way. Surely the best results were likely to come when the band was at ease with their surroundings. What better place than their own rehearsal loft, and what better man than their very own sound engineer, Dave Goodman.

> DAVE GOODMAN: *[The Spedding session] just happened and next time we got together Malcolm said, "Oh, we've got this tape we did. Have a listen and see what you think." It was at Majestic Studios and it just seemed so big and the band seemed lost in it. I listened to the tape and I thought I could do better on my four-track, being quite confident. I'd been recording [my own] eight-piece band on it. So I was challenged to bring it over to their Denmark Street rehearsal room which was a nice small room and run the cable upstairs and put the mixing desk on Steve's bed . . . We spent a*

21

week recording the first six tracks that [eventually] went on the Spunk album.

Goodman's personal brief, when he arrived at Denmark Street on the second Tuesday in July to begin recording the new set of demos, was to represent the sound they were building up to live.

> DAVE GOODMAN: *When they were relaxed and all in tune with one another the spirit of what they were expressing really came through in the music. Terms like "turgid" and "terse" were used to describe their music. It was a question of capturing that [but] . . . when we went on to record "Anarchy [in the UK]" for EMI at Wessex the reason why it was recorded so many times is that it never captured for me what I was experiencing at a good gig. They might be playing to ten, fifty people but it was a very clear, loud sound with a lot of psychedelic effects. All sorts of effects going on, you can hear it on the live tapes. In the studio it was only a three-piece band but you could overdub the guitars so it still sounded like one guitar but with all these high harmonies in there, dubbing on [things like] crash chords, which were things I [liked to] do.*

Setting up was not a problem. This was the quartet's rehearsal space (Jones and Cook were in fact living there on a semipermanent basis). The four-track with which Goodman had been recording his own band was hardly the Majestic console. It afforded little opportunity for mistakes, especially because two channels were already assigned for the vocal and guitar overdubs. Two tracks (one left, one right) to lay down a backing track meant it had to be live, with precious little chance of splicing between takes. Thankfully, the Pistols were now as tightly wound as a new Rolex. Goodman, however, was far more demanding than Spedding when it came to hitting the right groove, a groove he had already seen acquired before unknowing eyes. Goodman was aware that this might be no two-day affair.

> DAVE GOODMAN: *I was so analytical about a good groove and rhythm tracks that the first time they played it without any mistakes, they were going, "Do we need to do it again?" "Yeah, the groove, the feel, try it slowed down," whatever it took. . . . We spent a week,*

Monday to Friday [sic.], recording those demos, but that was just recording the backing tracks. Then we went to Riverside Studios and transferred it onto an eight-track and put on lead vocals and a couple of extra overdubs. And then we went to Decibel Studios and mixed it and probably put on a last few overdubs, like a kettle on "Submission," and things like that.

The absence of studio clocks meant that the Pistols did not need to be quite so picky about which songs to record. Because the only cost was tape (though McLaren seemed to resent even this small expense), seven of the band's double-digit repertoire were recorded that week in Denmark Street in some finalized form. These included one song less than a month old, "I Wanna Be Me," and one less than a week old, "Anarchy in the UK." The largely forgotten "Did You No Wrong," the best of the Spedding demos, "Problems," and "New York" were the only originals not attempted.

If "I Wanna Be Me" and "Anarchy in the UK" share an indignant rage, they are applied to very different targets. "Anarchy," taken at an almost sedentary pace compared with the *So It Goes* performance barely a month later, preferred handclaps to the usual atonal backing vocals. Rotten's vocal, however, conveys a barely contained menace. He clearly felt that this was as close to a message song as he had yet come.

The "Anarchy" vocal presumably comes from the overdub sessions at Riverside Studios at the end of July, not those at Denmark Street. As such, it had already been given its live debut at Manchester's Lesser Free Trade Hall, where the boys returned to a full house on July 20. Rotten was the only one at Denmark Street who knew he would get another shot. The final vocals would come "after the event," at the mixing sessions, which were already booked at Riverside in Hammersmith. But at this time, Rotten did not know the meaning of holding back, and, with the roar of the band filling his head, he blew the locks off of the life he had been born to. Goodman, unlike his successor Chris Thomas, preferred to record Rotten "live," perhaps a key factor in the mayhem-cum-magic evident on these tracks, along with the versions of "Anarchy" and "No Fun" recorded at Wessex in October.

DAVE GOODMAN: *One or two of the vocals that were done at Denmark Street actually ended up on the finished master but when he went home we [usually] overdubbed his vocal track with some guitar overdubs knowing that we were going to go into a studio with a Neumann mike and a compressor. That was one of the [problems], it wasn't easy to record without a compressor, but I do have the original four-tracks with a stereo backing track with one guitar overdub and a vocal. . . . [Rotten] always gave a good performance and a lot of his vocals were done in one take but there's also ideas, like, let's double-track his voice, and let's put a third track with a whisper over it [on "Satellite"] and [putting] effects like putting a long reverb on his voice on "Submission" [which required recording at Riverside].*

In fact, three of the original four-track versions made at Denmark, with their predubbed vocals, are credited as appearing on *Wanted: The Goodman Tapes.* The crude-as-two-star performances in question are "Pretty Vacant," "Satellite," and "Submission."

"I Wanna Be Me" was also a neatly trimmed debutante when Goodman attempted to harness it at Denmark Street. The success here of his technique for presenting the Pistols on overload (reminding one of that poor engineer's despairing cry at the Velvets' *White Light/White Heat* sessions: "All the needles are on red!") was such that the Pistols never felt the need to return to "I Wanna Be Me" in the studio, even though it remained a stalwart of live shows until the bitter end. This demo version even acquired an EMI label, as B-side to "Anarchy," despite or, perhaps, because of its obvious sonic flaws.

> DAVE GOODMAN: *Malcolm really liked the tapes and he tried to get them out. [On] "I Wanna Be Me" they just liked the guitar. That was just a question of overloading the line inputs on the mixer, which we used to do live. You get this real square wave distortion and you just blend it in with the guitar sound. On "I Wanna Be Me" we just turned it up full. In the studio, engineers would tell us you couldn't do it 'cause you might blow up the desk, but we never did.*

The other Denmark Street demo once due for official largesse was "No Feelings." It may well be the "true" anthem for the punk generation—a signature tune for the thief in the night with "no feelings for anybody else, except for myself, my beautiful self," casting scorn on "stupid fuckers, out looking for delight"—the Antichrist as common burglar. (It has long struck me that one possible source for the song might be a 1974 track by Sparks. Their breakthrough album, *Kimono My House,* uniquely quirky in conceit, contains a ditty entitled "Guess I'm Falling in Love with Myself Again," a true paean to the self-made narcissist.)

"No Feelings" would become the song the Pistols returned to the most. Even though Chris Spedding, Mike Thorne, and Dave Goodman all documented their notion of the song, the Pistols cut two more versions with Thomas and/or Price, one of which made it to *Bollocks,* the other of which was included as a bonus track on *This Is Crap.* What presumably inspired McLaren and/or the band to push for placing this demo on the B-side of the A&M version of "God Save the Queen" was not just Rotten's vocals-with-relish or that staccato intro that draws you in (a lesson surely learned from those two Mod kingpins, the Small Faces and The Who), but the audio-verité of a unit singular in purpose, stripped to the shell and rebuilt for public consumption. If the drums might as well have been Buddy Holly's cardboard boxes, the bass takes on the burden with muscle to spare, compounded by a couple of guitar overdubs that presage the "guitar soup" to come.

The maxim "technology is no substitute for creativity" has no better proof than the Denmark Street demos. The Goodman "Submission" may well be the most powerful moment the Pistols ever committed to oxides. From the high-end whistle (produced by a tea kettle, no less) that introduces the song, amid gurgles of delight from Rotten, to a riff kept simple from that master tea-leaf Steve Jones (chop the intro to the Kinks' "All of the Day and All of the Night" in half, slow it down half a measure, and voilà!), the song creates a world all its own, taking the listener down, down, down under the sea. Supposedly inspired by the one common musical ground Matlock and Rotten could agree upon—The Doors—no future attempt would ever surpass its July 1976 self.

THE ROAD TO EMI

With the demos all done, the Pistols took to the road again, playing anywhere they were allowed to lay Jones's Strat. The July Manchester show saw the debut of Mancunian punk progenitors Buzzcocks. A show in Sheffield unveiled The Clash. With The Damned also up and running, the UK punk vanguard was now primed for action-time-vision.

> DAVE GOODMAN: *It was [a matter of] delegation. Malcolm had no problem saying you book the B+Bs, pick the band up, here's a list of dates. We even had to put the money in the pot to go hire the van, to pay for the hotel, to get the money for the gig. If we could all arrive back in London with some money in our pockets [that was an achievement]. But at least we were a sustainable unit.*

If cracks were already starting to appear in this "sustainable unit," that high wire the quartet liked to dance on carried its own frission of tension each and every time they blasted through the rafters. If The Sound had arrived, Goodman's tapes delivered the proof. The fills that beefed up the four-tracks at Riverside Studio were calibrated on a whole other level to those slung on at Majestic. Sound for effect took the place of sound effects, even though Jones remained resolutely in the "Keef" camp, axemen with a riff to grind.

> STEVE JONES: *[Matlock]'d write these songs and play 'em to us on guitar and they sounded fuckin' diabolical. And he wanted me to play the same as him. Soundwise, the chords were jazz almost—*

*all minors and sevenths, wanky Beatles chords. . . . If he'd put
what he wanted those songs to sound like they wouldn't have sold
shit. Simple as that. . . . [The songwriting] really was a corporate
thing. (*NME,* August 19, 1978)*

As McLaren wheeled into action, with demos to play, there was com-
pelling evidence that the Pistols were more than mere hype. The Pistols,
after enduring one of the hottest Augusts on record, now began a sustained assault on media ears and eyes. At month's end, they made their
first (and only) live performance on English TV.

"So It Goes" was a late-night half-hour slot donated to Manchester TV presenter Tony Wilson by the local powers-that-be. Filling the program with the incongruous, the unsigned, and the unwashed, Wilson found only Granada, which held the franchise for Manchester and its environs, and London Weekend Television interested in screening it. No matter. It was not yet time to assault the heartlands.

Tony Wilson had been among the targeted few at the Lesser Free Trade Hall in June and badly wanted the Pistols on the show. Next time they passed through town the show was off air, and so in late August they had to be cajoled up the M6 one more time. The solitary song broadcast was their now-established call to arms, "Anarchy in the UK."

The "So It Goes" performance remains one of only two authentic visual indicators of the Matlock-era Pistols on full throttle. (The other was the November "London Weekend Show" punk special that Janet Street-Porter commandeered in order to show the Pistols lurching through the likes of "Pretty Vacant" and an abbreviated "No Fun," as well as interviewing the boys about impending fame.) Wilson's barely mouthed intro, "You can hear them warming up in the background even now," is all but drowned out by a sonic wail from the other side of Jericho, "BAYYBEE, a Woodstock kinda tenancy . . ." that dissolves into "Anarchy" just as Rotten bellows, "Get off your arse!!" All monitors except Rotten's fail in that moment, causing Jones to kick his redundant mike off the stage, and by song's end the stunned audience has been galvanized, delivering its verdict via a hail of chairs, two of which landed near the gyrating Sex employee, Jordan. The final shot is a closeup of Emperor Rotten, impervious to the caterwauling mob, caught in a stare from the depths of contempt. The "So It Goes" performance convinced one noted record producer to investigate these boys a little further.

> CHRIS THOMAS: *I went to see them, along with three million people, at the Screen on the Green. [Spedding] phoned me up. It was almost exactly the same night they were on "So It Goes." I said, "Where they on?" He said, "Islington." I said, "Where's Islington? I'll watch it on the telly." I saw it on the telly and it was like Mel Brooks's* [The Producers], *where the audience watch the first ten minutes [in] total silence, and it sort of had that effect on me. I thought I'm going to Islington tonight and got in a cab and went straight over there.*

Thomas's memory is playing tricks. "So It Goes" was broadcast six days after the Screen on the Green show, which took place on August 29 (at midnight, after the cinema shut down). But evidently the impact of seeing the band live and on TV so close together left a deep impression. Many consider the Screen on the Green to be the Pistols' finest live performance. Galvanized by the pretenders propping up the bill—Buzzcocks and The Clash, both making their London debuts—and Rotten being in mortal agony through most of the set as a result of ramming the microphone into his gob during "Anarchy" and knocking out his two front teeth, conspired to drive the boys onward and upward.

> CHRIS THOMAS: *In the context of the time it was really gobsmacking. I [actually] thought The Clash were better. With the Pistols it was just shellshock, I don't remember any great musical merit coming out of it, it was just a weird event. The thing I remember about The Clash [is that] they just seemed to have this row of guitarists.*

Two days later, the Pistols were back at a now-packed-out 100 Club, where The Clash once again performed for the dog-collared early birds.

And so to September 1976, the month when the Pistols played three of their most fabled performances: Chelmsford Security Prison (a crude soundboard tape, with the bass overdubbed, of this supposedly killer gig was issued in the late 1980s but the skewered mix all but neutralizes the drama of the occasion); the 100 Club Punk Festival (as headliners, of course); and the 76 Club in Burton-on-Trent: "A lot of speed / is all I need." The entire band on these tapes sounds wired to hell, roaring out redemption from shame in one Noise, "Noise, the grand dynamism, the audible expression of all that is exultant, ruthless, and virile—Noise which alone defends us from silly qualms, despairing scruples, and impossible desires. We will make the whole universe a noise in the end"—Thus spake Screwtape (C.S. Lewis, *The Screwtape Letters*). The Pistols were becoming impossible to ignore, even to those using their expense account "chits" to clog up their ears.

The 76 Club in deepest Derbyshire would have been just one more backwater on a map of lost gigs were it not for one hardy soul, cassette recorder in hand, who captured the veritable eye of this September storm. Four days after the Pistols had put the hex on the first and only 100 Club

Punk Festival with an "Anarchy" encore of cathartic feedback versus authentic urban hollering, the band still seemed to be riding its wave as it kicked off with "Anarchy" in Burton. And it never let up: "No Lip," "No Fun," no choice. The legendary bootleg *Indecent Exposure* first gave the world a glass-against-the-wall insight into the Pistols that night, but it could have been any night really. Through the autumn, the Pistols rode the sine waves for all they were worth.

Three days later Nick Mobbs, a man with access to an all-important checkbook—EMI's—decided to give the boys another hard listen (he had been at Screen on the Green), checking them out in the more sedate pastures of Loughborough University. Mike Thorne, Mobbs's junior at EMI at the time, had been getting on Mobbs's case, urging him to "Sign these guys up, whatever your personal doubts, sign these guys up." Still unsure, he stayed up all night listening to the Goodman demos until the morning brought illumination. If Mobbs knew that Polydor was about to propose a deal, he was presumably unaware that McLaren had convinced Polydor to cough up money for a session at De Lea Studios, to prove just how good the Pistols could sound in the studio. The session never happened. On October 8, the Pistols finally signed a record contract with the most English of labels, home to The Beatles: EMI.

THE FIRST
ANARCHY SESSIONS

McLaren had achieved his initial goal: getting a major record company to market his "protégés," even if EMI was hardly putting the crown jewels on the liene. Despite the unprecedented coverage this unsigned band had generated in the national music press, the Pistols' advance was a mere £40,000, payable in two chunks, a year apart. However, McLaren knew the time had come to stop making demos and start making records. EMI may have signed the Pistols, but they seemed to have almost no idea what to do with them. The choice of debut single was never in doubt, at least as far as the band was concerned. It had to be "Anarchy in the UK." (EMI apparently would have preferred "Pretty Vacant.") The Pistols were also angling for their own man as producer, Dave Goodman, who had met Mobbs back in September, when he had played him the Denmark Street demos.

> DAVE GOODMAN: *I met Malcolm and we went down for a meeting with Nick Mobbs. We sat and listened to the tape and, [he was like,] "Oh, yeah, overdubs in there. Oh wow, they're much more musical than we imagined." They must have felt fairly comfortable. I was an older generation "muso" and could sit and talk in their terminology about the production of a simple rock band. . . . [Malcolm] presented me as a possible producer who'd managed to come up with these tapes which [he] felt . . . captured something there, and developed a bit of a sound.*

That Goodman was given first stab at capturing that raging glory for real—on Studio Time—may partly be thanks to EMI's general uncertainty as to what to do with their newly acquired property. They clearly wanted the Pistols' debut 45 out while they were still deemed newsworthy. Goodman and the Pistols thus convened at Lansdowne Studios a mere three days after McLaren signed that dotted line on their behalf. For the first session they were accompanied by American rock photographer Bob Gruen, who seems to have encouraged them to make posing, not music-making, their first priority.

> DAVE GOODMAN: *We went to Lansdowne and we were in there for four days. I think they didn't want us back because John Magic Markered the walls and [anyway] it wasn't quite happening in there. So we moved to Wessex.*

> GLEN MATLOCK: *Dave Goodman . . . produced the demos which impressed EMI enough to sign us so we thought, fine, let's use him to produce "Anarchy." Malcolm wanted Dave to do it and Dave wanted Dave to do it. We thought: Give it a shot. First we went into Lansdowne Studios. It was our first time in a big studio. . . . We thought they were lucky to have us there—although they didn't quite agree with that. But that's the attitude we adopted and it's a good one. If you're trying to record something while you're feeling intimidated by the technology, it's not going to come out right on the tape. We had a week in there [sic] and it still didn't sound right by the end of the week. We played it again and again and again, pretty well most of the time, we thought. But nobody could make up their mind. There was no shortage of bodies around to venture an opinion. Malcolm was there a lot of the time. So were [photographer] Ray Stevenson and Dave's partner Kim Thraves. Loads of people but no one who knew enough about music to know what was great and who had the bottle to say, "That's it, that's the one, we can all pack up." We moved on to Wessex Studios.*

Wessex was soon to become a home-away-from-home for Johnny Rotten, Steve Jones, and Paul Cook. In the middle of October 1976, however, the switch from Lansdowne to Wessex did not yield immediate results. As Goodman and the boys wracked up a week at Wessex, EMI began to get more than a little nervous about what might be going down on tape. Or not.

> DAVE GOODMAN: *EMI couldn't understand how we spent ten days trying to record "Anarchy," which was like a three-minute rock song. [I was trying] to get a rhythm track that was worth building on. . . . But no one [there] really knew what a producer did. Like Glen said in his book, they needed someone in there to know when to stop. But that was me and it really was a case of like, "No, we still haven't cut it." It was a pulse [I was looking for]. [Sometimes] when you're under the spotlight you think too much about it. . . . I'd never really met anyone from EMI. They'd send people down and we wouldn't let 'em in. The band threw water over one guy. [EMI] were going, "What's going on?" . . . I just thought, "Record everything, this might be the album here." We'd just done "Anarchy" so many times, [so I] put it in the middle of a couple of songs, put it in the middle of the set. And everything would be really good and they'd get to that point and it'd not quite make it, something would slow down or something'd be a bit off and I'd say, "Okay, let's have a break, let's get something to eat." So we'd go down the pub and we'd come back and do a[nother] set. They had rostrums and they could all see each other.*

In his autobiography, Matlock is quite critical of Goodman's approach even though they worked together in the eighties on the *Concrete Bulletproof Invisible* EP. Matlock suggested that it was Goodman's inexperience in such a big studio, and an annoying perfectionism that refused to recognize how takes might be stitched together, that would ultimately necessitate a different producer, and a third attempt to confine "Anarchy" to seven inches of vinyl.

> GLEN MATLOCK: *We were getting remarkably cheesed off. The song wasn't sounding any better. In fact it must have been getting worse. Dave was casting around for things to alter. He—and Malcolm—started trying to get us to play faster and that was a disaster. As I've said before, this ran counter to what we considered the Pistols' sound to be about. . . . There must have been lots of times during*

that week when we did play it exactly right but still no one had the guts to say, "Yeah, that's the one." We were wasting a fortune in recording time. Plus Dave was using up reel after reel of two-inch tape, at God-knows-what a reel. On some of the reels were the other songs we'd knock out when we got bored—the great version of "No Fun," for example. . . . But most of the tape was just stuffed with attempts at "Anarchy." . . . John was really getting frustrated. He'd turn up in the evening and give us a hard time. "Haven't you done it yet? You're fucking useless, you lot. The papers are right, you can't even play. I never thought I'd believe The Sun.*"*

If the tapes made that week at Wessex have long been filed away, the sense of frustration that was eating at the Pistols can be heard on at least three of the covers recorded at Wessex, later appearing, overdubbed à la *Bollocks,* on *The Great Rock & Roll Swindle,* that double-album death rattle from 1979 for The Sound That Was. (The pre–guitar soup versions of the six covers on *GR&RS,* with Matlock's authentic basslines, plus a hilarious attempt at the Creation's "Through My Eyes" from the same sessions, can be found on the *Pirates of Destiny* CD.) As examples of "the other songs we'd knock out when we got bored," the versions of "Johnny B. Goode/Roadrunner" and "Whatcha Gonna Do About It" vividly convey the general torpor. Their release in the winter of 1979 was the kind of eavesdropping-as-permanent-record that allowed one of the *NME*'s terrible twins, Julie Burchill, to insult all-comers:

[The] six-minute jam session, man . . . seems at first to be a petty, oh-so-petty attempt to discredit J.R. until the singer stands alone as the only member of the band who doesn't come across like a brainless oaf. They begin, unbelievably, with "Johnny B. Goode," Rotten's screaching of a stream of frantic gibberish broken only by the occasional reference to "Downiner-Noo-Or-Leens," before breaking off and bemoaning the horror of it all. He tells Steve Jones to stop playing but he doesn't. He swears at Steve Jones to stop playing but he doesn't. He swears at Steve Jones but he still doesn't stop, carrying on his junior league, fat zero axe hero guitar wanking in sweet oblivion, very ignorant indeed, a real cretin. Even in those great days Jones just wanted to jam on that good old gui-

tar of his. And it was into these oafish mitts that the name The Sex
Pistols was to pass?

When Rotten roars out at the end of "Johnny B. Goode," it is certainly no expression of joy in the performance. Rather, he hits the nail on
the head with his cry, "It's horrible . . . the pits." "Stop it, it's awful," he
pleads, suggesting that they switch to Jonathan Richman's "Roadrunner,"
a song they had once flirted with at rehearsals. Unfortunately, Rotten is at
a complete loss as to the words, though his blank monotone rant, "der-
der-der, der-der-der" just complements the inarticulacy of the musicians
at this point. "Whatcha Gonna Do About It" is even more stripped of purpose, having been dropped from the set back in June. Rotten and the
guys launch into the song with enough gusto to suggest a long-forgotten
chestnut restored to glory, but they quickly tire of the task, and Rotten
reverts to a persona familiar to anyone who had seen the PA pack in, a

fight start, or the band break down at a Pistols gig, tearfully mocking the whole process, "I'm overwhelmed, oh it's all too much." As the song falters at the well, a spark ignites inside Rotten's mind as he realizes that only one song, nay anthem, can truly express the mind-numbing boredom, the sense of routine-become-rut, that they all feel, and he calls out to Cook, "Hey Paul, what about 'No Fun.'"

And suddenly, the band's tired limbs are energized, Rotten's previously langorous tones give way as Cook pounds out that simple, two-timing beat, and Rotten approaches the lectern, "WRRRRITTTEE! Here we go nOW! A sociology lecture with a bit of psychology, a bit of neurology, a bit of FUCKOLOGY! Nawww funnnn . . . I maybe going out / I maybe staying home / I maybe call somebody on the telephone / No Fun . . . I'm alive! No Fun!" Rotten opines on behalf of all the aspiring pond slime of Finsbury Park, seeking a bright, clean day. "No Fun," all seven minutes–plus, is exactly what Goodman had been striving for, that "pulse" acquired when thought processes are bypassed, when self-awareness is on mute, when there is just sound and fury. "Substitute," "No Lip," or "Steppin' Stone," other main-set mainstays that were part of the Wessex marathon, sound okay in isolation but fatigued in comparison to their natural state (i.e., live). "No Fun," a song that usually heralded the final assault live, captures the insolence of a Sex Pistols performance better than any other studio recording.

It was evidently Goodman's idea to erect a live setup at Wessex, where everyone could see and hear the other attendant components of sound. This suggests that he was not as far from understanding what was required as Matlock suggests. Indeed, if EMI had issued the version of "Anarchy" recorded at Wessex with Goodman, double A-sided with "No Fun" (as a story in *NME* in early November 1976 suggests the label at one point intended to do), they would have been responsible for perhaps the most radical debut in the already-jaded chronometer of rock.

From Rotten's opening retort, "Words of wisdom, right. Vinyl quotation number one," Goodman's "Anarchy" threatens to well up from beneath chugging riffs, disarming fills, and vocals barely retreating from the outer limits of dementia. Layer upon layer of feedback forces itself through the treacle-thick rhythm, to finally overwhelm. Whether or not the single would have sold, with Goodman's "Anarchy" (accompanied by "No Fun") comparisons would have been rejected before fermentation:

Outfeedbacking The 'Oo, outgrunging the Stones, outwailing The Stooges, the Pistols would have emerged reflected by studio technology, not refracted through it. As it is, the full seven-minute "No Fun" couldn't be fitted onto a seven-inch single at 45 rpm. Rather than issue a twelve-inch version, McLaren just told the cutting engineer to cut it off at 6.32, as the B-side not of "Anarchy," but of "Pretty Vacant."

The Goodman "Anarchy" wouldn't officially appear until *The Great Rock & Roll Swindle,* where it appeared alongside several tired Wessex covers (though not "No Fun," which sadly continues to reemerge in its 6.32 guise, except on the fifteen-track *No Future UK* set on Receiver, where it can be found wails'n'all). On *The Swindle,* Goodman was able to release the mix that he wanted. "Anarchy" has the roar of one very pissed (off) lion, the din of a legion of feedback-merchants, and the thrust of a ship with Captain Ahab at the helm and the big Dick in his sights. Unfortunately, it was not this mix that, after a week at Wessex, was presented to the jobsworths at EMI as a potential debut.

> DAVE GOODMAN: *John's vocal, 'cause he'd sung so much, was really rough and should perhaps have been the guide vocal but part of me was saying, "I like it really rough like that." . . . Unfortunately Mike Thorne was a young A&R guy at EMI who was somehow involved in what we were doing, and after we did the rough mixes, he began talking to Glen [Matlock] about how he thought the production was going, and everyone was asked to leave and I was asked to rough mix it up. I'd decided that "Anarchy" was going to be the heaviest piece of music I'd ever heard and that was it, no question about it . . . [but] Mike Thorne went in with Glen and did a remix and they cut an acetate of that and that's what they played to the A&R department at EMI who started throwing doubt on whether it cut the mustard. Mike Thorne did the mix. . . . They should have let me sleep it off for a few days and let me get back in there and carry on working.*

THE MIKE THORNE SESSION

Some dispute has arisen over what happened after EMI rejected Goodman's "Anarchy." At some point, Mike Thorne took the Pistols into EMI's own Manchester Square studio, while Chris Thomas rerecorded "Anarchy in the UK" at Wessex, the version that EMI would finally sanction for release. Goodman seems to think that Thorne shot his own bolt before ushering Thomas in. In *Sex Pistols Day by Day*, Lee Wood dates the Thorne session after the single's release, but attributes a version of "Anarchy" to this session, begging the question: Why would the Pistols rerecord a song they had just released? The use of Manchester Square's studio casts further shards of doubt. It was hardly state of art, being no more than a basic eight-track setup intended largely for recording publishing demos for EMI's music publishing arm. Thorne, a junior A&R person in 1976, would hardly have been entrusted with capturing the definitive "Anarchy," and certainly not in one of EMI's demo studios.

In fact, a four-song tape circulates from the Thorne session, and it is quite obvious that these are demo recordings. Nor is "Anarchy in the UK" part of the quartet. The tape, which was broadcast on an Italian pirate radio station back in 1977 (and therefore has an annoying Italian presenter talking over all four intros) comprises "No Feelings" (backing track only), "No Future," "Liar," and "Problems." (The Thorne recording of "No Future" has circulated separately, minus DJ verbiage, on the *Aggression thru Repression* bootleg CD.) These recordings are attributed to the last two weeks in December 1976, that is, during the all-but-aborted "Anarchy" tour. An EMI press release of December 6, 1976, stated that "future recording plans are to make a new single at the end of

December for release in February 1977. It is also planned to record an album in January for release in March/April." A session completed by EMI's A&R man to produce demos for potential followup singles makes an awful lot of sense. Which still raises one question: Who were the demos for? For the producer, Chris Thomas? (Unlikely.) Or was this a subtle attempt to "vet" the Pistols' next single?

If so, a few palpitations must have greeted song number two at the next EMI sales meeting, listed on the tape as "No Future" but soon to be better known as "God Save the Queen." Did such a song further convince EMI to jettison these misfits even if the "punk" controversy clearly equaled record sales ("Anarchy" had, after all, charted before being banned)?

The presence of "No Future" on the Thorne tape argues against a post-Goodman, pre-Thomas recording date. According to Matlock, "The main riff was something I found piddling around on the piano, while we recorded the aborted version of 'Anarchy.'" Rotten had already written the words, in a single stint, and was surprised when they fit "with the pattern that Glen had." The song was given a live debut at Hendon Polytechnic on November 19.

If the four Thorne tracks were contenders for the next Pistol 45, not surprisingly "No Future" was the least focused. The remaining trio had all been doused in the furnace of tinpot clubs. The Thorne "No Future," fascinating as the only real example of a Pistols work in progress, requires a major overhaul. Minor flaws aside, the song on the Thorne tape clocks in at an unheard of 5.10, repeats its second bridge ["When there's no future how can there be sin? . . ."], contains a most un-Jones-like, meandering guitar solo, and has a "no future" chant at song's end that almost takes on "Hey Jude" fadeout status. It also contains one of Rotten's most embarrassing rhymes, "God save the queen / God save Windowleen," ranking alongside "I am an Anti-Christ / I am an anarchist." "No Future" was badly in need of some pruning shears.

"God Save the Queen" in its released form would be a triumph of feeling over meaning. As a set of lyrics, it descends into nonsense, abounding in non sequiturs ("Lord have mercy, all crimes are paid"— Huh?) and muddled conundrums ("When there's no future, how can there be sin?"). Yet ultimately, it still Conveys [capital C] a sense of the postimperial malaise paralyzing Britain circa '76 in a way pretenders like The Clash and The Jam could only aspire to.

But the Thorne "No Future" hardly suggested *Single*. "Liar," on the other hand, with its prototypical Pistols intro and "blah blah blah" lyrics, might yet have made a teen anthem/vinyl quotation number two. As it is, the Pistols still had a debut single to promote, the result of their first workout with Chris Thomas, an old vet at EMI, whose first-ever productions, uncredited, had been at those tortuous wind-downs to The Beatles' studio career, *The White Album* and *Abbey Road*.

> CHRIS THOMAS: *The first Beatles stuff I did was* The White Album. . . . *Originally [I was] just sitting at the back doing nothing, just watching and learning but then [George Martin] went on holiday for three weeks and . . . I ended up doing . . . quite a few songs while he was away. I think they'd only done about ten songs in three months and in that three weeks we did like seven songs. When we did "Happiness Is a Warm Gun," I believe we went over a hundred takes on that and edited between two. . . . When it came to* Let It Be, *I didn't go down to many of those sessions, I never went to Twickenham at all, then they sort of petered out and they went back to Abbey Road and everything seemed to meander along. Then they started doing more new stuff and that sort of became* Abbey Road. . . . *I remember Paul sitting down in Abbey Road No. 3 and playing me this whole thing which lasted about fifteen minutes, it goes into this and into that.*

THE SECOND
ANARCHY SESSIONS

But it was not his work with The Beatles that commended Chris Thomas to the Pistols. Nor was it his work on that most reviled monument to ProgRock, Pink Floyd's *Dark Side of the Moon,* where, in Thomas's own words, "I came in at the end of it." Even this did not apparently tip the balance against him, counterweighed as it was by his work on John Cale's *1919* and five of the first six Roxy Music albums, notably the marvelously atmospheric *For Your Pleasure.* However, the crucial record in his C.V. was perhaps one of Thomas's most obscure assignments ever.

> CHRIS THOMAS: *I don't know about John but the other three had heard a Kilburn and the High Roads record I'd made and they knew about my Roxy stuff, and they especially liked "Rough Boys" [by Kilburn]. It was on Pye. 'Cause it was one question I asked them was, "Why'd you want me to do it?" [Originally] I didn't even get to meet John. The whole thing was almost done behind his back. It was very strange. I'd met Malcolm because he was talking about managing the New York Dolls and me producing them.*

> GLEN MATLOCK: *Paul . . . came up with the idea of using Chris Thomas as a producer. I wasn't that familiar with his work but Paul was really into Roxy Music, who Chris had produced. He played a few of their albums to Malcolm. Now I'm sure Malcolm couldn't tell what he was meant to be listening for—production is such an*

44

ANARCHY IN THE U.K.

SEX PISTOLS

FIRST SINGLE
EMI 2566

See them live at
SAT 4 DEC   **DERBY** Kings Hall
MON 6 DEC   **LEEDS** Polytechnic
THU 9 DEC   **MANCHESTER**
             Electric Circus
FRI 10 DEC   **LANCASTER** University
SAT 11 DEC   **LIVERPOOL** Stadium
FRI 17 DEC   **SHEFFIELD** City Hall

intangible thing . . . [but] whatever Malcolm thought about all this,
he said, "Okay, let's try Chris Thomas."

Although Thomas had seen the Pistols at the Screen on the Green when Rotten, in particular, was on fire, the attendant distractions of a circuslike atmosphere, the usual PA problems, and cramped conditions meant that the strength of the Pistols' songwriting had largely passed him by. However, when Mike Thorne approached him about the possibility of producing the Pistols, he agreed to hear some tapes.

GLEN MATLOCK: *We—minus John, who hadn't deigned to come—*
went round to Chris Thomas's house in Ealing. His wife, an
absolutely gorgeous Japanese woman, was there as well. We
already knew her, as she was one of the Sadista Mika Band and

was always coming into Malcolm's shop when it was [called] Let It Rock. He seemed pretty interested in working with us. He'd heard what we'd done and liked the song ["Anarchy"]. Great chord changes, he said.

CHRIS THOMAS: *I got a call from Mike Thorne asking me if I could produce them, so we fixed up a meeting and three of them came to my place. John didn't come, I don't even know if he knew anything about what was going on. And I heard the demos and that was the point, I mean the demos of stuff like "Pretty Vacant," it was like this is a great British rock band in the tradition of say The Who, guitar-bass-drums-vocal. Some of them might have been [the Goodman demos], some of them were Spedding demos. . . . It wasn't so much the quality of the demos, it was the songs. "Pretty Vacant" is just a brilliant song, brilliant riff, one of the great rock riffs.*

It is extremely unlikely that Thomas was played any of the Spedding demos, which had long been consigned to the scrapyard. He must have been played the "rough mix" of Goodman's "Anarchy in the UK," as Matlock strongly implies. For starters, the band would have wanted Thomas's thoughts on why, and in what ways, the process might be defeating them, and what ideas he might have for shaking things up.

GLEN MATLOCK: *A couple of days [after our meeting] we were in the studio with [Thomas]. We moved that fast because there was already a release date scheduled for "Anarchy" and no one wanted to lose the momentum of all the press we'd generated. Again we were in Wessex. . . . We spent a morning setting up, making sure the sound was right. Bill Price, Wessex's engineer, did that, thinking of tiny little things which would improve the sound. For instance, he picked up a metal flight case and set it at an angle by Steve's Twin Reverb amp to give a better reflection of the sound, producing a slightly harder edge. This was a real attention to detail which we'd not had before. He also set up a couple of ambient mikes, to record all the peripheral sounds in the room. When you mix that in with all the other music it gives you a bigger, more immediate, and "liver" sound. It makes the tracks sparkle. And so we started playing, running straight through five takes. That took* us up to about four in the afternoon. Chris said, "Oh, I think we've got it there, let me just try this." He took the first half of one take and the second half of another and spliced them together, then played us the result. It worked. The only thing wrong was a slight timing discrepancy on the snare drum during one of the verses. They got round that by rigging up a tape delay to double the snare pattern. That made a blemish into a feature. And, hey presto, we had one cracking rhythm track. All we needed was John to add the vocals. Where was John? He rolled up about seven. "I suppose you lot haven't fucking done it yet," he said. "Punk rock, that's you all over. You're useless, you lot, you can't play." "OK, then clever clogs," we said, "you just get in there and sing. We've done it." "What do you mean you've done it?" "We've done it. Just like we've been saying all along, we've been playing it well enough. All it needed was somebody to realize when it was good enough. Now it sounds great." John did his vocals and, after a couple of days' break, we went back in to do some overdubs—extra guitar from Steve basically. But I started sticking my oar in. "I'm the guitarist," Steve, said, "why don't you sling your hook down the pub and let me do it?" . . . When I came back from the pub Steve had finished his overdubs. Then Chris Thomas mixed it with Bill and it was all finished.

According to Goodman, in an interview with Chas De Whalley of *Sounds* back in 1977, "EMI were a bit put out that we hadn't done what they wanted and they said the production wasn't good enough. So they brought in Chris Thomas, who really only copied my demos note for note but made them into pop records." Thomas refutes Goodman's version of events.

CHRIS THOMAS: *I certainly didn't refer to [Goodman's] version particularly. It was quite the reverse. The crime that I committed—that I got slagged off for quite a lot—was I introduced them to the world of overdubbing loads of guitars. I came up with all these extra bits, like having the feedback running through the last verse. There were like sixteen parts in there, well maybe eight or ten, which was a typical thing that I [like to] do.*

Even the most cursory of listenings to Goodman's and Thomas's versions of "Anarchy" does not bear Thomas out. The notion of getting Jones to "layer" various guitar parts goes back to the July demos, and in particular the Riverside sessions, after the original four-track was transferred onto eight-track. If Thomas singularly failed to replicate the footstomping middle eight that announces that last verse of Goodman's version, the "feedback running through the last verse" very audibly originates on Goodman's "Anarchy." Although Thomas considered the sound he ended up with to be "much closer to The Who than The Ramones," it is the Goodman "Anarchy" that bears that particular legacy best. If Goodman observed few pop conventions, Thomas overlooked few of them.

Where Thomas had succeeded was in recording the basic track quickly and with a minimum of fuss, something Goodman had singularly failed to do. Thomas also got a sound that EMI could be happy with. Booked back into Wessex the last week in October, the Spikey Foursome had managed to complete the job in less than forty-eight hours, and the single remained on EMI's Christmas schedule.

The most obvious way that Thomas betrayed roots in the George Martin School of Record Production was in his approach to recording Rotten's vocals. First, there had never been any question of trying to cut a live vocal. Second, when Rotten attempted his usual bellowed vocal, Thomas felt the need to coach Rotten into getting the words across loud and clear, using tone, not volume. Of course, Rotten was used to having to shout at gigs just to be heard. The last gig prior to this session had been at Birmingham's Bogarts club. Rotten's vocals are almost entirely absent from the live tape save for heartstopping moments like the one in "Pretty Vacant" when the band desists and Rotten gets to holler, "And we don't care!!!" Or in "I Wanna Be Me" where the false ending always invited shouts from the audience, before Rotten could signal a resumption of play with, "Down, down, down, down . . ." At gig's end, Rotten's voice had all but packed in, and, even with the weekend break, Thomas could hear the ravages of another bad PA on Rotten's vocal chords.

CHRIS THOMAS: *I think they were a bit confused about what was going on. They were in the center of [all this media attention]. There was so much happening. After doing the backing track, when John came in to do the vocal he just started to yell through it and I thought it was really important that you could hear the lyrics. I worked really hard on that in terms of editing it from various takes to make sure that you can hear it, and I made the voice quite clear. Again a thing that was criticized. . . . At the end of it, when we were mixing it, the others were crashed out upstairs but John stayed in the control booth the whole time and when it got to the end of the mix he said, "That's our anthem," and he was obviously happy. Which meant that I'd finally broken the ice with him, 'cause I think he viewed me with great distrust as some kinda tool of the record company. It's the hardest thing, working on any record. It's got to be on complete trust. I know at the end of it they were really happy. It sounds really menacing. I know it doesn't go at 150 miles an hour like The Damned, which was another criticism Richard Williams pointed out, [but] to me it was much closer to The Who than The Ramones.*

Unfortunately, the more Rotten tried to sing—forgetting that his forte was "getting it across," not hitting notes—the more detached the results tended to sound. In Public Image Limited, Rotten's later group, and indeed in the recent Pistols reunion, a singsongey falsetto sometimes intrudes on the blackest of sentiments, transforming the Antichrist into a Cockney Tiny Tim. The single as released does indeed get the words across loud and clear; whether it gets the gut feeling across is another question.

Thomas also decided that a little more brevity might be in order. On the Goodman "Anarchy" the final coda, "I wanna be, anarchy" [*sic*] threatens to overwhelm the song itself as the band is wound up to the nth. They are four minutes in before they are finally released from sonic cave-in by Rotten's "I wanna be an anarchist—get pissed—DEE STROY!" Cue subsiding waves of feedback. On Thomas's take—all 3.02 of it—it almost sounds as if the plug has been pulled at song's end, so abrupt is the climax. According to Thomas, he actually *wanted* a genuine form of sonic destruction to signal the finale.

CHRIS THOMAS: *When we cut it at EMI, I wanted the very last noise so [loud] that the needle jumped in the air and mashed your needle up. I wasn't allowed to do it by EMI. The very first person to play*

*it was John Peel, and then the Peel voice comes over the air, "I
was hoping maybe the record needle might leap up in the air at
the end!"*

What few criticisms that were voiced against the attendant results in the
English music press tended to center on the orthodox poppiness of the
Pistols' debut, not the dense guitar sound or the lack of sneer. Given that
the most anodyne of versions of "Anarchy" would sound like Catharsis
Inc. compared with the kind of Manfred Mann–Muzak then casting its
counterfeit reflection on commercial rock, the reviewers were always likely to give the Pistols the benefit of the doubt. Caroline Coon, a fully paid
up member of the inner circle of punk journos, reviewed "Anarchy" for
Melody Maker. Hardly a dispassionate observer, she set her hype-pen to
eleven:

> They scrapped the first try at recording the single after an abortive
> weekend where good fun and liquid refreshment flowed to the
> detriment of music. They re-recorded it with Chris Thomas pro-
> ducing. This time they were meticulous and their care and atten-
> tion pays dividends, totally destroying the myth that UK punk rock
> revels in untuned instruments and sloppiness. . . . Rotten enunci-
> ates every word with the clarity of a branding iron. It's great. It's
> startlingly harsh, loaded with cynical irony and too concerned with
> urban reality to appeal to those settled into the thrill of romance.
> But for restless young renegades bored with sugar and spice
> images, which are about as far removed from the life they know as
> Venus and Mars, it will be an instant hit.

Sounds refrained from giving the single to their own voice from the
sanctum sanctorum, Jonh Ingham. Alan Lewis still made it "Single of the
Week," waxing lyrical about how, "by any standards, it's a great rock
record." However, he also recognized some concessions to the mainest of
streams—chartdom: "Pistols fans, I suspect, will be surprised (disap-
pointed?) that the record isn't faster and nastier. It's just a little too
smoothly produced by Chris Thomas of Roxy Music fame. . . . No, this
ain't revolution, it's the same old rock & roll—but YOUNGER and more
intense than we've heard it for a long while."

ANARCHY IN THE U.K. TOUR

SEX PISTOLS

FIRST MAJOR
U.K. TOUR WITH
SPECIAL GUESTS **THE DAMNED**

JoHnny THunder's HeART BreAkers

(Ex New York Dolls from USA)

THe CLaSh

TOUR DATES

Tickets From

Date	Venue	Tickets From
FRI 3 DEC	**NORWICH** University	Students Union, U.E.A.
SAT 4 DEC	**DERBY** Kings Hall	Kings Hall, Derby
		R.E. Cords, Derby, Burton Slect a Disc
		Nottingham Record Centre, Long Eaton
SUN 5 DEC	**NEWCASTLE** City Hall	City Hall
MON 6 DEC	**LEEDS** Polytechnic	Village Bowl
TUE 7 DEC	**BOURNEMOUTH** Village Bowl	Students Union, Leeds Poly
		Hime & Adamson, Manchester
THU 9 DEC	**MANCHESTER** Electric Circus	Virgin Records, Manchester
FRI 10 DEC	**LANCASTER** University	Students Union, Lancaster University
SAT 11 DEC	**LIVERPOOL** Stadium	Virgin Records
MON 13 DEC	**BRISTOL** Colston Hall	Top Rank, Cardiff
TUE 14 DEC	**CARDIFF** Top Rank	Buffalo Records
		Colston Hall
WED 15 DEC	**GLASGOW** Apollo	Apollo, Glasgow
THU 16 DEC	**DUNDEE** Caird Hall	Caird Hall
		Students Union, Technical College
FRI 17 DEC	**SHEFFIELD** City Hall	City Hall – Wilson Peck Records
SAT 18 DEC	**SOUTHEND** Kursaal	Usual Agents
SUN 19 DEC	**GUILDFORD** Civic Hall	Usual Agents
MON 20 DEC	**BIRMINGHAM** Town Hall	Town Hall
TUE 21 DEC	**PLYMOUTH** Woods Centre	Virgin Records
		Woods Centre
WED 22 DEC	**TORQUAY** 400 Ballroom	400 Club
SUN 26 DEC	**LONDON** Roxy Theatre Harlesden	Roxy Theatre

SINGLES AVAILABLE

THE DAMNED. NEW ROSE HELP (BUY 6)
Available from even your dumbest dealer
SEX PISTOLS. ANARCHY IN THE U.K. (EMI 2566)
Available from your cleverest!

TOUR PRESENTED BY
ENDALE ASSOCIATES
IN ARRANGEMENT WITH
MALCOLM MACLAREN

NOTORIETY BECKONS

Friday, November 26: the release date for the debut single by a band much heralded in Britain's self-enclosed music press, but all but unknown to anyone more than one step removed from their brand of cutting-edge rock and roll.

Friday, December 3: The Pistols are due to embark on what had been planned as the first punk package tour, "Anarchy in the UK." To publicize the event, they appear on a teatime TV show hosted by Bill Grundy, who shamelessly provokes them into uttering a series of expletives. Now, only the most hermitlike residents of this sceptered isle remain unaware of these "foul-mouthed yobs," so christened by Grundy. A barely audible "shit" (from Rotten), a "dirty sod," a "dirty bastard," one "fucker," and a solitary "fucking rotter" (all from Jones) took the Pistols in a single week from vinyl quotation number one to Public Enemy Number One. Grundy, who tried to fob the blame on to the band, ended up losing his job anyway.

For the "Anarchy in the UK" tour, McLaren had hijacked New York's favorite junkies, the Heartbreakers, along with the two most proficient UK punk combos, The Damned and The Clash, hoping to reinvent that quaint form of yesteryear, the package tour. The schedule rapidly imploded as censorious councillors—self-elected spokesmen for that nebulous creed, the Moral Majority—applied to the max. their powers to revoke music licenses. Directing their glare at any establishment willing to offer these punks shelter from the storm, they set out to prove that freedom of speech was just another phrase from the Politicians' Dictionary of Humbug.

The only venues exempt from the long arm of local councils were the three "homes of higher learning" on the schedule. Even Norwich and Lancaster Universities preferred to take the hassle-free option, leaving just Leeds Polytechnic and two venues located in boroughs where the local councils were unwilling to abuse their prerogative powers—Manchester and Plymouth—as sole survivors of an original nineteen-gig schedule. Shows in Cleethorpes and Caerphilly, and "bonus" shows at Manchester and Plymouth, padded one of the most legendary rock tours out to seven dates (the same number as the Pistols' one and only U.S. tour), performing for no more than a couple of thousand of the convinced and converted.

Having signed to the most English of labels, the Pistols suddenly found themselves victims of that most English of social diseases, the hypocrisy of elders. Their little TV tête-à-tête had come at a most embarrassing time for the EMI record division. On Tuesday, December 7, obliged to address their annual general meeting, the chairman of the board, Sir John Read, strongly hinted that the Pistols' tenure at EMI might soon be up:

> Sex Pistols is the only "punk rock" group that EMI Records currently has under direct recording contract and whether EMI does in fact release any more of their records will have to be very carefully considered. . . . Our view within EMI is that we should seek to discourage records that are likely to give offense to the majority of people.

The few forces at EMI in favor of hanging on to the most exciting British band in years probably knew after Read's statement that they were fighting a losing battle. Despite Mike Thorne's bringing the boys into HQ to cut some demos, the band and their novice manager were isolated figures at Manchester Square, and their single, which reached the lower end of the charts the week after the Grundy kerfuffle, was no longer available. The blue-rinse brigade at EMI's Essex pressing plant had discovered that a single called "Anarchy in the UK" actually preached anarchy in the UK!

LAURIE HILL [MANAGING DIRECTOR, EMI]: *Because of the outrage in the press, there were ladies at the factory who said, we aren't going to handle the records. And they refused to handle the records. Now*

that was why the records weren't available for some time. Because you know with a thing like a single, you don't know how many you're going to sell and you have to react very quickly to demand. And because the ladies refused to handle the record, um, we couldn't supply it for a time and so shops didn't have it.

Having signed to EMI largely because they had the distribution, the Pistols found that a chart single was being made deliberately unavailable—perhaps the first single ever to be deleted (in all but name) while still climbing the charts. By the end of the "Anarchy" tour, the Pistols realized the time was fast approaching when they would have to take their wares elsewhere. McLaren, having realized the jig was up, thought he might get EMI to cough up some more funds so that the boys could get back to Wessex to cut their own little brand of consolation. Five days after the "Anarchy" tour spluttered to its conclusion on the doubtless-windswept shores of a December Devon, the powerpop trio of Matlock–Jones–Cook scheduled a day with Thomas and Price, hoping to cut some backing tracks. Thomas insists that Matlock was absent from this Boxing Day session and that the

Jones/Cook power duo ended up cutting basic tracks, entire and complete, for the next two Pistol 45s, the very singles that would galvanize a generation waiting to fill in the blank. (Boxing Day, which usually comes on the December 26, came on December 27 in 1976, the 26th being a Sunday.)

> CHRIS THOMAS: *I can't remember when they got turfed out of EMI, but we'd already started recording more stuff 'cause I remember we went in on Boxing Day and Glen had been kicked out of the band [sic], but was invited back as a session musician. Not surprisingly, he didn't turn up. So . . . on Boxing Day afternoon, it was just Steve and Paul. We did "Pretty Vacant," "EMI" [sic], "God Save the Queen," and something else. It was pretty weird without a bass player. You just got Steve and Paul. [So we] just put one of them down, didn't seem to be any mistakes there, we did another one, and I think at the time we were [still] waiting for Glen to turn up.*

Although there is no doubt that a session took place on Boxing Day 1976—Glitterbest secretary Sophie records in her diary for December 27, "The band are doing backing tracks today"—Thomas has surely telegraphed the events of two distinct sessions, making them into a single day's work. (For the band to have recorded the song "EMI" two weeks before they got hoofed off the label would have been prescient indeed.) We are wholly in the dark as to what songs may have been attempted at this session. However, Matlock was still very much a part of the setup, and a no-show from Glen would have warranted comment from Sophie in her private diary, which was later published as part of Fred and Judy Vermorel's history of the Pistols, *The Inside Story* (Star, 1977).

THE GOOSEBERRY SESSIONS

What is certain is that Boxing Day at Wessex was the Pistols' last session as members of the EMI roster. On January 4, the Pistols flew to Amsterdam for a three-date Dutch tour. While they concerned themselves with internal wrangles and much name-calling, EMI considerately issued a press statement on their behalf:

> EMI and the Sex Pistols group have mutually agreed to terminate their recording contract.
>
> EMI feels it is unable to promote this group's records internationally in view of the adverse publicity which has been generated over the last two months, although recent press reports of the behaviour of the Sex Pistols appear to have been exaggerated.
>
> The termination of this contract with the Sex Pistols does not in any way affect EMI's intention to remain active in all areas of the music business.

It had been a decidedly unmutual agreement. In fact, McLaren had informed the music press prior to the band's departure for Holland that "the band had no intention of being bought off by the record company." By the time he and the band returned, on January 8, it was a done deal. The Pistols came away with £30,000, £20,000 of which comprised the other half of their advance, and the remainder a payoff from an earlier publishing contract with EMI Music. Since they were not even interested in retaining the traditionally lucrative song-publishing rights to the Pistols, EMI was saying in Words Writ Large, "We want nothing to do with these

EMI was saying in Words Writ Large, "We want nothing to do with these Cockney slubberdegullions."

Despite the absence of any obvious outlet for a record bearing their imprimatur, the Pistols were once again ushered into a studio at McLaren's behest just ten days after their unceremonious dumping by EMI. Thomas, though, was no longer in charge of the technical side. Rather, the Gooseberry sessions marked the return of Dave Goodman.

> DAVE GOODMAN: *[Malcolm] was off to Paris. I was still working with the band. "Book a studio for the weekend, get their minds off things, they've got some new songs." Gooseberry Studios. It was mixed down later at Eden Studios. They'd only just got the sack. There is some film from those sessions. NBC had been sent over to film the Pistols. They came in, spent an hour filming the band. A few more overdubs [were done at Eden]. . . . [Malcolm] did express [the opinion] that this was the album that should have come out.*

Goodman's presence at the console over four days in mid-January raises a whole slew of questions: If the Pistols were pissed off at Goodman for his failure to capture "Anarchy" on tape, why restore him to favor now? *Uh, who else?* Since the band had been in the studio with Thomas since "Anarchy," where was he? Why was Wessex Studios suddenly, if temporarily, out of *Uh, cost,* favor? What was the "true" purpose of cutting these tracks, at least in McLaren's scheme of things? How many questions are there to a slew?

The truth, as per usual, may well be explained as different shades/disparate factors. Clearly, McLaren still had a great deal of faith in Goodman's instincts, and given his continuing involvement as soundman on the "Anarchy" tour, so presumably did the band. The factors that had worked against Goodman at Wessex—an attack of nerves on the band's part, unrequested outside interference, and the imposing twenty-four-track Wessex console—were absent from Gooseberry. Thomas's association with EMI, though he had long enjoyed independent status, may have temporarily soured the band to his virtues, while Wessex may simply have been too demanding on McLaren's rusty bankbook.

It would be just like the old days—no label, no future. And when McLaren said, "they've got some new songs," he was not telling Norf

London "porkies" [pork pies=lies], even if the five-month old "Liar" was one of the "new" ditties. More brand-spanking-new was "No Future," the lyrics now honed and willing to face the music, while—still in its wrapping paper—was another box of bile by the name of "EMI."

The Gooseberry Tapes represent a halfway house between the demos-in-the-attic approach of the Denmark Street demos and the wealth of distractions that was Wessex. Sixteen-tracks gave Goodman enough rope. He could assign Cook's powerhouse drums the tape-width needed to confirm his status as a one-man engine room, while Jones's increasing penchant for multi-dubbed guitars might be held in some kinda check by the need for a couple of vacant bands of tape for Rotten to impose his will at overdub stage. Matlock, though fast becoming disenchanted with the continual sniping of that most inverted of snobs, frontman Rotten ("No man who says I'm as good as you believes it."—C.S. Lewis), tagged along to play his part in one last drama: the recording of "God Save the Queen." The riff to this song may have been his baby, but he had refused to play it as an encore at the Pistols' final show in Amsterdam ten days earlier.

Of the six tracks the Pistols cut at Gooseberry with Goodman—taken in order: "Pretty Vacant," "God Save the Queen," "Liar," "EMI," "New York," and "Problems"—"God Save the Queen" is the crown jewel. Interestingly enough, Goodman had only previously recorded one of these songs, "Pretty Vacant." This was the superior version destined for *Spunk*. "God Save the Queen" sounds like a song written by a bassist, its burbling bass line playing tag with the Jones chug, making for one undiluted riff-o-rama. Rotten also veers between studied drawl and untutored rant with all the self-confidence of a master ham, while Jones this time prefers filling out the sound to filling up the tracks (a loose riff at song end is one such great discard). If there had been any doubts that "God Save the Queen" could cut it as a single, Gooseberry banished them for good.

But at these sessions a certain antsiness also occasionally sneaks through. On the *Spunk* bootleg, the intro to "Pretty Vacant" has Jones joking, "I hoped we passed the audition." This was not just a nod to Lennon's January 1969 rooftop retort, but an admission that he perhaps felt they'd done enough audition tapes. At the end of "New York," Rotten dismissed the song with what sounds like, "I'm getting tired of fucking abaht [that's Cockney for about]." Thankfully, that antsy quality, when fed into the music, does wonders. Not surprisingly, "EMI" is delivered with the sort of venom that, if it could have been liquidized and snuck into their afternoon tea, would have meant adios EMI board, chairman et al. With Matlock again providing the song's hook, Rotten's delivery makes it crystal clear that here is a man who knows defeat in battle ain't about to signal the cessation of hostilities.

The Gooseberry sessions also proved that the "Anarchy" sessions with Goodman were an aberration, a compound of everybody trying just a little too hard. The sessions at Gooseberry took just four days, January 17–20; Goodman returned from a weekend in Cannes to complete the overdubbing and mixing on the January 24 and 28, though not until secretary Sophie had settled the studio bill, "Because the guy won't let the tapes out till that's done."

Whether McLaren and/or the band ever intended the Gooseberry tracks to be more than just demos attendant upon some future record deal is now perhaps a moot point. None of the cuts appeared on *Bollocks,* or even as Virgin B-sides, despite McLaren's abiding belief that Goodman had once again captured some aspect of the Pistols' sound permanently absent from Thomas's sea of possibilities. At least one Gooseberry track was certainly played for A&M British boss Derek Green during negotiations begun with that label.

"No Future" was one of eight tracks Green heard the following month, along with "Pretty Vacant" (again probably the Gooseberry version), "No Feelings," "Submission," and "Anarchy in the UK" from the July tapes, Goodman's Wessex "Anarchy," and Thomas's single of "Anarchy." Curiously, an article by Tony Parsons in *New Musical Express* on May 21, 1977—entitled "Blank Nuggets in the UK"—suggests that as late as the signing to Virgin, the Pistols' still envisaged their debut album as a mix'n'match of Goodman and Thomas–produced tracks:

> The album is produced by Chris Thomas (who acted in the same capacity on the EMI "Anarchy in the UK" single) and Dave Goodman of The Label label, who produced the B-side of that single, "I Wanna Be Me."
>
> I heard the acetate of the Dave Goodman–produced tracks that are already in the can round at Dave's flat.
>
> The first thing he played me was the version of "Anarchy" cut before the one chosen as the single. This earlier take is the one

which will be on the album, and is infinitely superior to the single; Rotten's sneering, belligerent vocal tirade is more up front, the lyrics spat out with more venom. Cook's drumming, Matlock's bass line and Steve Jones's guitar all come through with more raw power than I've heard from the band since last summer. . . .

But this track is certainly not alone in coming across on that level of excitement, tension and, yeah, quality.

There are also killer versions of "No Future," often misnamed "God Save the Queen" . . . [and] another song called "EMI" [which] doesn't contain the reference to A&M included at the Screen on the Green gig, but sticks instead to their view of the uneasy partnership and of why they had to part company. Rotten's voice is full of undiluted hatred. . . .

More black-hearted blank nuggets are the ex-Doll David Johansen parody, "New York," a long version of Iggy's "No Fun" (the only non-original [planned] for album inclusion), the B-side of "Anarchy," "I Wanna Be Me," a great version of "Submission," an okay version of "Liar" and a fine recording of the vastly underrated "Satellite (Suburban Kid)." . . .

And that leaves just one cut on an album that seemed for a while as though it would never appear, an album that will divide opinion more radically than any rock album ever released, an album that makes me believe it ain't inevitable that the ideals of the New Wave in the '70s must go the same way as those of the previous generation. The remaining cut is "Problems." Rotten sings, "An' the problem is YEW!"

GOD SAVE THE QUEEN, VACANT, AND A&M

Presumably, Derek Green was aware from the outset that the Pistols intended to release "God Save the Queen" as their next single. Certainly, by the time the Pistols officially signed to A&M on March 9 the wheels were well in motion for single number two to be "God Save the Queen" b/w "No Feelings." According to A&M's press release—a self-congratulatory pat on the corporate back for foresight above and beyond—the Pistols' first single on A&M was scheduled for release at the end of March.

By the time McLaren signed up for another letdown, Goodman's "No Future" from Gooseberry had once again been superseded by a Chris Thomas version of the same track. This time Thomas delivered the goods, one three-minute timebomb, even though he began work at a substantial disadvantage. The Sex Pistols no longer had a bass player. By early February, Matlock had had enough and decided to inform *Melody Maker* himself, a week ahead of an "official" announcement: "I've been getting a load of needle for ages, and since the [Anarchy] tour I knew it wouldn't last. It was mainly friction between me and Johnny. On stage he's great but he'd carry all that into the rehearsal situation and I couldn't handle it." *NME* and *Sounds* ran stories the following week reporting that the Pistols had sacked Matlock.

Matlock's replacement would prove to be an extraordinary choice: Sid Vicious, a member of the Bromley Contingent, a group of wannabes without the wherewithal (Siouxsie of the Banshees excepted). Vicious had been rehearsing with other stray punks unable to slot into an existing setup in an amorphous body called The Flowers of Romance, named after the Pistols' cacophonous take on "Booker T," but as a bass player he was at ground zero. The combustible cocktail that made the Pistols tick-tock was being tampered with largely at Rotten's behest, over the sort of spats that Daltrey and Townshend had been having in The Who for a dozen years or more. Matlock remained as integral to the Pistols' sound as Townshend was to The 'Oo. Moreover, the UK punk milieu was not so well formed that bassists with the innate musicality of a Matlock just skulked among the habitués of SoHo, awaiting release. Unlike Television, who could afford to dispense with their songwriting bassist and visual focal point and emerge the stronger, there were no contenders for the bass slot in an unsigned band with an egomaniac for a singer, an "unmusical" reputation, and who had just self-evidently displayed a worrying lack of awareness of their own strengths.

When McLaren signed Matlock's final check he was signing the band's death warrant. What remained was a nine-month-long death rattle. The media circus had only just begun, and, if Rotten had removed Matlock to ensure that the focus of the band remained firmly on him, the plan backfired bigtime. Rotten was far too cynical to buy into the punk myth he had helped unravel. Vicious, however, was a truly volatile mixture of naivete, stupidity, and self-absorption. Rehearsing with Vicious was a waste of time, as Jones and Cook quickly realized. With sessions for their next single fast approaching, they spent two days in early March at their Denmark Street rehearsal space working with Vicious, trying to teach him the straightforward bassline to "God Save the Queen."

On March 3, with an A&M deal all but agreed, the newly reconfigured Pistols scheduled two days at Wessex, with Chris Thomas once again producing and Bill Price as engineer. However, Jones and Cook knew better than to try to fool all the people all the time. Discounting Rotten's feelings, they asked McLaren to persuade Matlock to make a temporary return to the fold. This was the Matlock-as-hired-hand session Thomas mistakenly attributes to Boxing Day 1976, and it came about because Sid Vicious, Matlock's (cough) replacement, was simply not up to playing bass parts in the studio. According to Jon Savage, "Matlock was kept on to do an audition session on March 3, for which he was paid, along with

the agreed settlement fee." However, this was no audition session. The A&M deal was a *fait accompli*.

> GLEN MATLOCK: *In late February 1977, [McLaren and I] met in The Blue Posts [on Hanaway Street], a pub behind the 100 Club and had a long discussion. . . . [McLaren] told me that they were going to do some recording—obviously for A&M, although he didn't say anything to me about that at the time—and asked me if I would help out because Sid wasn't too good. I agreed.*

Not surprisingly, Rotten's version is more embroidered; one might even say fanciful.

> JOHN LYDON: *Sid wasn't very good at recording. . . . Sid was too fucking drunk, quite frankly. It was desperation time, so in came Glen. We literally hired Glen Matlock. What a nice touch! Shame on him, he actually did it. Isn't that awful? That, more than anything tenfold [sic], explains my contempt for him.*

Save for one thing, Johnny: Glen *didn't* turn up. He seems to have only agreed on condition that he was paid up front. He was presumably angry over the cajoling and threatening previously required simply to get money due him. He then pocketed the dosh (your dosh, Johnny) and skipped out on the session.

Not that Rotten was even in attendance that day. This was a session for laying down basic tracks, after all. That Matlock's no-show was unexpected and unwanted is quite apparent from Sophie's diary entry for those days, "Thursday and Friday, band in the studio, chaotic apparently, everyone hating Chris Thomas. Steve doing bass, guitar overdubs, back up vocals, the lot!" Thankfully for the future of the Pistols' album, Jones took to his new role as the bass player behind the curtain with an aplomb that surprised even Thomas.

> CHRIS THOMAS: *[When it was obvious] Glen wasn't going to show up, I said to Steve, "D'you wanna have a go putting some kind of bass line on it so that we can start work on it," 'cause I couldn't kinda conceive of carrying on with anything without that. I remember saying to Bill, "Take it, just in case he comes up with some odd idea, an accidental thing." I imagined sitting down and having to work for four hours on the part for one song, and all he did was play the root note of the chord that he was playing all the way through and Bingo! you immediately had that sound. "Anarchy" was different 'cause it had Glen on bass but once it got to this thing where Steve played this root note, that's what really galvanized it. Suddenly you just had from this very simple three-piece line-up this Panzer Division, so I got him to put bass on the other three songs. So that's the point, Steve played bass on everything [on*

Bollocks] except "Anarchy" and I think "Bodies." . . . What happened on "God Save the Queen" was that they got Sid in to play bass but it was so crappy, it might [still] be there as a rumble underneath, but it's Steve on bass. I never did anything with Sid [again], it was so out of time and sounded pretty crappy. I think it's mixed in but with Steve playing the percussion of the note.

The four songs cut on the March 3 were apparently "God Save the Queen," "Pretty Vacant," "EMI," and another (perhaps "Did You No Wrong"). "God Save the Queen" and "Pretty Vacant" were then over-dubbed by Rotten on the fourth and mixed on the spot. The team of Thomas and Price were now, once and for all, assigned production duties and work began in earnest on what would become the Pistols' already long-awaited debut album.

If, as Thomas has implied, the version of "EMI" cut on the March 3 proved to be the master take, at least in basic track guise, the vocal on *Bollocks* (and indeed on the alternate "EMI" on *This Is Crap*) is not one (if any) that Rotten dubbed on the fourth. The final line, "Hello EMI, Goodbye . . ." lacked one more word, the name of another record company.

Completing the single versions of "God Save the Queen" and "Pretty Vacant" in a two-day session puts the March 3–4, 1977, Wessex sessions in contention for two of the most productive session dates of the modern multitrack era. In the one-two combination stakes, what two consecutive 45s stack up against this combo: "Can't Explain"/"Anyway, Anyhow, Anywhere"?; "Jumping Jack Flash"/"Honky Tonk Woman"?; "Complete Control"/"White Man in Hammersmith Palais"? Now you're struggling.

"Pretty Vacant," though it would have to stand in line in order to become a Pistols 45, defines the Pistols' teen-rebel stance without any attendant politico-pretensions. It takes its place in an honorable tradition that connects everything from "Blue Suede Shoes" through "It's My Life," "My Generation," "Satisfaction," and "Blank Generation" to "(Smells Like) Teen Spirit." And, like all of those songs, its declamatory style is presaged by a riff lifted from Lucifer's top drawer. Running relay, Thomas gets the perfect twelve-second intro out of Jones, before passing the baton to Cook who, twenty seconds on, lobs it as far as Rotten, who sounds well and truly "out to lunch" as he revels in the notion that a song about a VAY-CUNT office might define the stance of a generation of fellow teen-rebels.

DANCE TO THE SEX PISTOLS

 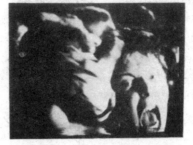 

WE'RE SO PRETTY   OH SO PRETTY

VACANT

AND WE DON'T CARE

NEW SINGLE

OUT NOW ON VIRGIN RECORDS VS 184

SEX PISTOLS

W.H. Smith's Top 20 Elephant and Castle. June 13th.

BBC RADIO ONE
Banned. "It is in gross bad taste" Charles McLelland. The ban covers the whole of the BBC.

WH SMITH
Banned at all branches.

Banned. The nations' Brewers have refused to allow Sex Pistols on any of the Juke Boxes.

Banned at all branches.

IBA
Banned. "Nothing should be broadcast which offends good taste or decency. And that includes all radio advertising."

TOP OF THE POPS
Banned. "It is quite unsuitable for an entertainment show like Top of The Pops"

 LUX
Banned. And Luxembourg are independant of the BBC and the IBA. The ban by Luxembourg, the IBA and the BBC mean that the single is barred from every British radio station.

GLC & LOCAL COUNCILS
Banned. Sex Pistols are not even allowed to play in London or in most other parts of the country. And when they try to...........

Banned. A Thames River boat party was broken up by police on Jubilee Day. Fifteen people were arrested.

 LOCAL RADIO
Banned. No local stations will play the single.

 THAMES
Banned from advertising. Not even 'God Save The Queen', but simply the new signing with Virgin. And all the ad said was: "You thought you had got rid of us, but you haven't"

MEMBERS OF PARLIAMENT
"If pop music is going to be used to destroy our established instutions, then it ought to be destroyed first."
Lambeth M.P. Marcus Lipton

Banned. The Pistols were fired and "Anarchy in the UK" was withdrawn as it hit the charts.

 RECORDS
Banned. Just three days after signing.

ASSOCIATED PRESS
Banned. One of Britains' impartial Press Agencies has refused to circulate news stories about Sex Pistols.

SOUNDS PRINTERS
Banned. The printers, not the paper, deliberately ommited part of an ad for 'God Save The Queen' without informing Virgin or the Sex Pistols.

TONY BLACKBURN
"It is disgraceful and makes me ashamed of the pop world, but it is a fad that won't last, we DJ's have ignored them and if everyone else did perhaps they would go away."

JOHN PEEL
"One of the greatest Rock records ever made" (Sounds June 13th But the BBC won't let him play it.

 CAPITAL RADIO 194
Eventually, banned. But Capital were the only station in the country to question the IBA ban. And 'God Save The Queen' made their Number One slot.

MELODY MAKER, SOUNDS, N.M.E. & RECORD MIRROR ✓
Sex Pistols 'God Save The Queen' is record of the week.
'God Save The Queen.' No.1 in NME thanks to you and England's independant record stores. Support real record shops.

"God Save the Queen" (GSTQ) could never be half the pop classic that "Pretty Vacant" was, but as a statement it was one Molotov cocktail tied to a stopwatch. Thomas must have worked fast to ensure that GSTQ would be fit to appear on the first A&M seven-inch. The importance of releasing a statement like GSTQ at a time when the Queen's Silver Jubilee was painting over gaps-cum-chasms in the threadbarest of Western economies (two years down the line the chancellor of the exchequer would have to go to the IMF, cap in hand) may be a tad hard to convey twenty years on. "God Save the Queen" was not about a woman called Elizabeth Windsor but about asserting a right to a future that a redundant establishment (on Liz's behalf) seemed determined to deny. With Rotten encapsulating the rage of the inarticulate classes, Thomas needed to muster all available resources to bring out each loaded threat ("we're the poison in the human machine / we're the future, your future") every malignant curse ("they made you a moron / potential H-bomb"), until passion itself kicks down the barricades that surround closed minds.

This time Thomas captures Rotten's genie and puts in the cork. Jones zooms in and out, bouncing from track to track, to bass and back, but "God Save the Queen" is Rotten's baby. Although Green (and presumably the A&M A&R team) had heard the song "No Future" before drafting a contract for the boys to sign, perhaps they had not heard Rotten's vision with Thomas at the helm—that is, until it was too late. Five days after Rotten's vocal filled up the last remaining track on the two-inch tape, the Pistols signed to A&M. I would like to think it was listening to this single-to-be over the following weekend that caused Mr. Green to think, "What have I done?"

> DEREK GREEN: *It wasn't primarily their behavior, it was what their behavior created. The reaction to their behavior. That's what concerned me.*

Even though it took Green all of four days to regret his decision to sign the Pistols, terminating their contract at a meeting with a bemused McLaren on March 16, several thousand A&M singles were pressed up and had to be quickly destroyed. The band name alone had halted the presses once again. Inevitably, a handful of A&M's pressing of "God Save the Queen" snuck through the net, though only a handful, and it is now one of the most valuable of vinyl collectibles (the last reliable estimate I heard: around $3,000!).

The Pistols were in danger of experiencing at first hand the veracity of Jesus' notion of Judgment Day, when "many that are first will be last and the last first." The year 1977 was indeed Armagideon Time. There was certainly never any question whether the Pistols were the original seditionaries. But were they now being left behind? The Clash's debut 45, "White Riot," hit the stores the day the A&M deal fell through. In a punk résumé written for the unaware that appeared in *Sounds* at the beginning of April, the Pistols were lauded as the founding fathers of the punk movement:

> Credit where it's due—none of this would've happened without the Pistols. And they produced one of the best singles of 1976, as well as ever-improving live shows which gave the lie to the old "they can't play" criticism. Annoying though that they haven't done a show in months and that the A&M deal collapsed. Not to mention dangerous from the point of view of the number of fans who'll ultimately get sick of waiting for the Pistols to materialise and place their allegiances elsewhere. Still, maybe longevity isn't part of the master plan.

That sense of impermanence—the feeling that a return to the status quo might just be around the corner—always attendant to the whole punk explosion, also bore the brunt of its hidden charms. The volatile nature of seventies youth culture gave many their fifteen minutes, but tame seventies-style could prove a most capricious bitch. The period between March 16 and May 13, when the Pistols finally ceased to be refugees from the record industry, reluctantly signing with those "bloody hippies" at Virgin Records, must have been a dark time for all concerned.

THE PRICE IS PAID

Despite the failure of the A&M deal, McLaren decided that the boys should proceed full steam ahead with a Sex Pistols album. The eternal optimist, he believed that any time lag between deal and album would be minimal. Unfortunately, label after label rejected McLaren's overtures until, on April 22, came the biggest blow of all: Polydor—the label that had been duking it out with EMI for the Pistols' signature just six months earlier—confirmed that it was no longer interested in offering the band a contract.

In late April/early May, while McLaren hemmed and hawed about the only real offer on the table—from Virgin Records' head honcho, Richard Branson—Rotten, Jones, and Cook turned their minds to making a long-player. On May 6, while McLaren was signing the Pistols to a deal with Barclay Records for France and an adjoining territory or two (a shrewd move that subsequently allowed him to play a few mind games with Branson), Sophie the secretary reports "go[ing] up the studio—good as always to see the band. Watch Steve doing overdubs on 'New York' & Bill Price getting the best bits out of four. Amazing."

Price's role in the recording of *Bollocks* was to prove at least as important as Thomas's. As the chief in-house engineer at Wessex, Bill Price was a technician first and foremost. Whether the Pistols, or rather Jones and Cook, needed the input of a producer, particularly a "hands-on" producer like Thomas, at this point is highly debatable. A twelve-month tour of London studios—taking in the likes of Majestic, Riverside, Lansdowne, Wessex, Manchester Square, Gooseberry, and Eden—had left little need for further tricks of the trade, particularly with songs already honed to a chrome sheen in licensed beer pits up and down the land. Indeed, Jones would subsequently dismiss Thomas's contribution to the sound of *Bollocks,* telling *NME* on August 19, 1978:

> Thomas done nothing. I'd double-track everything. I even played the bass on nine tracks [on *Bollocks*—actually ten]. . . . It's our sound. No-one else's. It's easy for us to get, 'cos we're playing. Like, to me . . . I use a lot of echo, right, and Phil Spector's my inspiration as a rock producer. So what I wanted to get was a new wall of sound.

Cook, often little more than a bystander at the *Bollocks* sessions as Jones filled up track after track with his "new wall of sound," was considerably more gracious as regards Thomas's contribution, crediting him with the important role of devil's advocate, willing to push Jones into laying down one more coat of gloss. In the same issue of *NME,* he said:

> Actually, I think Thomas was fuckin' good—but then I was the one who chose him because I liked the sound he got for Roxy Music. But, like, the way we built up those tracks—it's something that's been overlooked—but it was both Chris and Steve . . . taking little bits that don't jump out at you, but they form . . . layers upon layers. . . . We were lucky, I reckon, choosing Wessex with Thomas and Bill Price.

Rotten also eventually came to feel comfortable with the gospel according to Thomas.

> JOHNNY ROTTEN: *Chris Thomas did a hilariously good job as producer of* Never Mind the Bollocks. *I liked the idea of using him because I liked Roxy Music, although I knew we would never sound anything like them. I didn't realize until we got in the studio that Chris was hearing impaired in one ear. He has engineers like Bill Price to tell him what's in and out of tune.*

Rotten, though, was less enamored of Steve Jones's seeming compulsion to fill up all twenty-four tracks, growing quickly frustrated by the process itself.

JOHNNY ROTTEN: *I was a bit bored making the Sex Pistols album. There was something like twenty-one guitars laid down and only two tracks for vocal—one for the verses and one for the choruses. I did most of the songs all the way through, one or two takes, and that's it. There was very little bouncing of tracks, and I got very annoyed.*

Jones had never needed a whole lotta cajoling to lay down a guitar track or four. It would be Jones, not Cook or Rotten, whose "one more overdub, just one more overdub" approach would push *Bollocks* further and further back on the release schedule.

STEVE JONES: *I loved recording the* Bollocks *album. I remember when I was doing some guitar overdubs late at night, I heard on the radio that Elvis Presley had died. I remember it clearly because . . . I just thought I'd better get back and do those guitar overdubs.*

Rather than being offended by Jones's statement that he'd "done nothing," Thomas is largely at one with Jones's view. In Thomas's eyes, the whole recording of *Bollocks* became formularized very quickly—shortly after the breakthrough session that resulted in "God Save the Queen" and "Pretty Vacant."

CHRIS THOMAS: *I remember the singles because I'd work on them in a completely different way. And I suppose I was definitely affected by the reception for "Anarchy," which was a bad reception from the critics, they really criticized the production, and I thought, alright, I won't do any of this overdubbing m'larkey and I cut it down to the bare minimum. I still cut Steve's guitar up in the mix, but if he put a track down I'd get him to doubletrack it, so you got two guitars, one on each side of the stereo, and then I'd pull out various bits and maybe we'd work on those. But it might only be three or four guitar sounds instead of nine or ten. Once this thing happened with the bass it gave it such a strong sound that it didn't need the bolstering up that "Anarchy" needed. But Steve really started to fly after this, "I wanna do this, I wanna do that," which was great but I remember at some of those sessions feeling a bit non-creative 'cause they'd rehearsed it so much. If I was working in the control room, Steve and Paul used to go out and just go thru the set, which lasted about forty minutes, basically the album, and then they'd go and watch a bit of telly, and then they'd go downstairs and go thru the set again, just simply to stave off boredom. So literally you'd get to the point where backing tracks would be take one. Then put the bass on and see if they'd made a mistake anywhere. But it always worked. So it became very routine. In the past, I always used to treat a song as a song and take it in whichever direction it would grow, whereas with this it was [like] the songs are like this, they're played like this and once we discovered the sound, the way to record the drums, and discovered various ways of miking everything up, basically it was very formularized. It was the first time I'd ever done anything formularized: We'll do the next one like the last one. The only thing that was distinguishing about the production was the guitar overdubs. The drum part was the drum part.*

For a man who had worked with the likes of Pink Floyd, Roxy Music, and John Cale, artists ever looking to sideswipe a track into a previously unforseen direction, the Pistols—with a defined repertoire, sound, and style—hardly represented much of a challenge, exciting as their songs may have been. In many ways, Thomas's role on *Bollocks* was similar to his role on another millstone of seventies rock, *Dark Side of the Moon*, where, in Thomas's words, "I came in at the end of it. With Roxy it was much more my stuff, my input." With *Dark Side*, Floyd had not only rehearsed the album as a whole, but taken the entire overblown shebang on the road. Recording and mixing the bestselling album of the 1970s was thus a very routine exercise—Thomas being the one called in by Floyd to supervise the final mix.

For much of the period preceding the Virgin deal, whether largely because of the "formularized" nature of the studio work or the depressing resistance that invariably greeted "that name," Thomas went temporarily AWOL.

CHRIS THOMAS: *There was one point where I didn't go in there. [I think] it was around the April or May time. [I] left Bill really to finish it off. They'd already been kicked off A&M. By the time they got*

NEVER MIND THE BOLLOCKS/THE SEX PISTOLS

*kicked off A&M it was getting very depressing: What's the point of
making a record that's never gonna get released?*

Thomas's recollection is that some five cuts on *Bollocks* were produced
entirely by Bill Price. Given that Thomas was on hand for all four singles
plus "Bodies" and, apparently, "EMI," that leaves the overfamiliar oldies-
but-goodies down to Price (i.e., "New York," "Liar," "No Feelings,"
"Problems," "Seventeen," and "Submission"). Thomas has no recollection of working on "Satellite," one of just two tracks to have taken up
Wessex tape but excluded from *Bollocks.* [Note: Neither "Satellite" nor
"Did You No Wrong" was entirely sidelined, being B-sided to "Holidays"
and "GSTQ," respectively.] "Satellite" would appear on just about every
preliminary track-listing *Bollocks* was to undergo.

Presumably, most of these songs were recorded at the late
April/early May sessions, with Price as sole technical overseer. (Sophie
makes no mention of Thomas in her May 6 diary entry.) On the evidence
of the final *Bollocks,* Price, if anything, gave Jones even greater latitude
to build his guitar-tower of Babylon. What Jones hoped to achieve with his
tiers of guitars may have been beyond Jones's repertoire of words, but
clearly a sound was bouncing around inside his head.

The danger in Jones's approach was perhaps first revealed on *This
Is Crap,* which, among its *Bollocks* alternates, contains a version of
"Satellite" that shares a suspicious kinship with the take previously available on *Kiss This* (i.e., the "Holidays In The Sun" B-side). The *This Is
Crap* version was presumably the mix that kept cropping up on pre-
release sequences for the album, before the decision was made to release
a fourth single and place "Satellite" on its B-side—i.e., before Jones
decided to work on the song just a little bit more.

The *This Is Crap* "Satellite" is actually the *Kiss This* "Satellite" minus
a few embellishments and mixed in the light of day. But after years of listening to the original release, the *TIC* "Satellite" comes as a revelation.
Cook's drums are resurrected from the mire. Even Rotten's end-of-song
bleatings now lie in the audible range, so he can be heard pleading, "I
can't take no more. Please stop!" as Jones scales another wall of sound.

The *Kiss This* "Satellite" is a quagmire buried in quicksand. Rotten's
vocals have lost their crispness, the drums have been subsumed by the
guitars, which have in turn been dolloped in mud. Rather than reveling in

a series of guitar subtexts, the listener senses only suffocation. (In fairness to Jones, a large part of this stems from the flaws of the CD medium; on vinyl, the compression required allows a certain partition of sound.) As a three-minute *volte face* to "Holidays," that sense of suffocation may not have been a problem. Translated to a long-player, it threatened to become a big problem. Jon Savage admitted with hindsight in *England's Dreaming* (he makes no such call in his original review in *Sounds*), "It is difficult to listen to *Bollocks* all the way through, [even if] individual tracks show the Sex Pistols at the height of their power."

Of course, none of these problems loomed as large as the fact that the group still lacked a label. McLaren needed to find someone willing to put out a Sex Pistols album. Turned down by the likes of Decca, Pye, Polydor, and even CBS—the label that had signed The Clash (and promptly overrode their wishes by issuing "Remote Control" as their second single)—McLaren was finally forced to arrange a meeting with his one remaining potential conduit, Richard Branson, owner and self-styled impressario of the Virgin Records roster. Branson's label had twice been dismissed as a possible producer of Sex Pistols records. Even as late as early May, with the Queen's Silver Jubilee fast approaching, McLaren was trying to do a one-off single deal with Virgin, hoping to up the band's premium for a long-term deal with a "major."

Branson was having none of it, however. When it came to business, he could smell a desperate man the minute his soles hit the shagpile. On May 12 the Pistols put their name to their third record contract, all save Vicious who was in hospital with hepatitis, the first of many signs that Vicious was buying into the whole sex, junk, and rock 'n' roll schtick. Along with their signature, the band brought a two-sided opus for immediate release. "God Save the Queen"/"Did You No Wrong" was to be available in select stores (i.e., those willing to stock it) just two weeks after they became a Virgin band.

THE PISTOLS ON VIRGIN

And lo! it came to pass that "God Save the Queen" came out in time for the Queen's Silver Jubilee. The collected ire of a nation could now be brought to bear on the Spiky Ones. Sure, there had been singles-as-statements before but never had the act of buying a record been such a "fuck you" to Trad. mores. *NME*'s Single of the Week review, after describing "GSTQ" as "a remorseless, streamlined crusher of a single that establishes the Pistols' credentials as a real live rock and roll band," appositely noted: "Anyway, buy it. Buy it whether you like The Sex Pistols or not. If people try that hard to stop you from hearing something then you owe it to yourself to find out why."

And buy it they did. And ban it they did. Banned by the BBC for "gross bad taste," and unstocked by branches of W. H. Smith, Boots, and Woolworth's (between them accounting for well over half the record outlets in the UK), the single was castigated by everyone from impotent have-a-cuppa OAPs to the nation's appointed lawmakers. In a one-sentence deconstruction of free speech, Lambeth M.P. Marcus Lipton opined: "If pop music is going to be used to destroy our established institutions, then it ought to be destroyed first."

It seemed that The Sex Pistols were asking for "it." Their ad for "God Save the Queen," designed by would-be-Situationist-looking-for-a-situation Jamie Reid, depicted the Queen with a safety pin through her mouth (in Reid's original version she also had two swastikas for eyes, but even the Pistols recognized some dangerous borders). If inciting the wrath of the neophobes was the game plan, in a country where the monarch was the state's intermediary to God (i.e., head of its very own

NOWHERE

Sex
pretty

state religion, the Church of England), that came very close to blasphemy. The week after "God Save the Queen" snuck into the independent record stores of Albion, the front page of *Melody Maker* was taken up with a large photo of a London "bobby" booking Johnny Rotten and Sid Vicious for walking down the street. The opening sentence of the accompanying story quoted Rotten's reaction: "This is called living in England in 1977."

The Pistols were back as the national tabloids' favorite bogeymen, criticizing what they could never understand. Meanwhile the music press remained the one outlet where the Pistols had a chance of getting their point of view across. Interviews in the semiconverted pop weeklies *Melody Maker* and *Record Mirror* in the first week in June sat on the shelves alongside a lengthy cover story in the now punkified monthly *Zigzag*, which had only recently abnegated its role as the last bastion of hippie music. "GSTQ" had just reached a highly suspicious number two in the charts. (A number one slot would have required the BBC to explain its omission from "Top of the Pops.") Virgin was selling 200,000 copies a week of "GSTQ," but Rod Stewart was somehow selling more—at least, in Boots, Smiths, and Woolies he was. Meanwhile, Rotten was once again reaching for the soapbox: "We're winning. Whereas in the past any band that has stuck its neck out has always backed down, we haven't. Never

PiSTOLS vacant

VS184 : OUT THIS SATURDAY ON VIRGIN RECORDS VS184 : OUT

will. That's the difference. And just as soon as it gets really boring is when I'm going to stop."

Asked how the album was going, Rotten saw fit to dismiss Thomas's input—"At the start he didn't know what the hell we meant. We said, 'Cut out all the Roxy Music bullshit. It's not what we like'"—while heaping praise on Price's contribution: "He understands straight away what you mean, which is what we want." Still refusing to come clean on Jones's role as the studio bass player, the boys insisted that bass duties on the album were split between Matlock ("on the Chris Thomas tracks") and Vicious. Progress on the album was "ongoing," however. Rotten admitted: "We understood it more this time. When we done 'Anarchy' it took fucking weeks. . . . We didn't know what we wanted. We each had a different idea of what it should sound like, so we just had to work it out."

They were back in the studio. On June 18, 1977, Jones, Cook, Rotten, and Chris Thomas, having returned to production duties, spent a frustrating Saturday with Bill Price working on the Pistols' first post-Matlock ditty, "Holidays in the Sun," when they decided to retire to a pub round the corner for a little imbibing. *& to celebrate Paul McCartney's birthday!*

CHRIS THOMAS: *It was a Saturday afternoon. We were working only weekends [on the album] because I was working [elsewhere] dur-*

ing the week, and Steve and Paul went down to the pub about six o'clock, and then I followed on with John and Bill. And John really looked like John. This was quite a notorious figure strutting down the street . . . then Steve and Paul left quite early, and John started saying, "Those blokes over there are gonna have us," and I was like, "C'mon John, don't be so paranoid, people don't go out on a Saturday night to have people, they go out to have a drink." . . . And we went into the car park and there was like a football team [of them], eleven blokes, and they dragged me off and I had a rip down the shirt, I got kicked to the ground, but apparently Bill dragged somebody off me who was lunging at me with a knife. So they took him round the corner and gave him a good kicking. There was like three guys and one knife, they were passing the knife. It was all over in thirty seconds and we tried to phone the police and they wouldn't let us in the pub. That happened on the Saturday, it was front page on the Tuesday. I went to work [at a McCartney session] and everybody had been scouring the hospitals. I just walked in, they showed me the paper, "Oh that was Saturday night."

There is something rather ironic about Rotten ranting on about holidaying "in the new Belsen . . . 'cause now I got reasonable economy," and then running straight into the UK bullyboy equivalent of the old Nazi brown shirts. "Holidays in the Sun," the perfect anthem for a summer of hate, took the bullyboys' big stick and beat them back: *"I didn't ask for sunshine and I got World War III/ I'm looking over the wall and they're looking at me."*

As Rotten was fond of reciting, "Just because you're paranoid, doesn't mean they're not out to get you." Tell the truth. "Claustrophobia . . . too much paranoia . . . I'm gonna go over the wall. Please don't be waiting for me." If "Holidays in the Sun" was meant to put the Pistols back on track, the whole country seemed to be derailing to the sound of "Naww phuchaw!!"

"Holidays" had made its live debut the first week in June, during the Pistols' abortive "riverboat gig." In a publicity stunt par excellence, the band played to the chosen few on a Thames pleasure boat the very day the majority of the country took to having street parties to celebrate another long-lasting member of the house of Windsor. As the Pistols warmed up the partygoers, the river police, donning their best partypooper gear, duly climbed aboard. A few cracked sternums later, McLaren, Westwood, the long-suffering Sophie, Jamie Reid et al. were in the local nick for disturbing the (fishes') peace—the Pistols themselves were not detained.

"Holidays," a new song on the continuing subject of who exactly "made you a moron/ potential H-bomb," highlighted the dense new sound now planned for *Bollocks:* Guitars to the left, guitars to the right, a Rotten rant stuck in the middle. "Holidays" also gave Thomas something to sculpt, an opportunity to ply his trade, configure the sound. Written by Rotten during a spring weekend in Berlin (having been first turfed off of the Channel Isles), "Holidays" had first been attempted in the studio with Price in May whilst still in its pure, Dadapunk state. Another "No Future"–style overhaul was required.

> CHRIS THOMAS: *Malcolm [had] contacted me and I [had] listened to what Bill had done. I remember thinking "Holidays in the Sun" could have been a single but the construction of the song was wrong and so we went in and redid that. There were verses in the wrong place, the solo was in the wrong place. It started off with a bass drum thing but I just had the idea of putting goosesteps on it because it was Berlin. Then of course you can't goosestep that quick and Bill Price came up with a great idea, he just recorded one on a tape loop and triggered it off the bass drum.*

Initially, the band did not share Thomas's enthusiasm for making "Holidays" into a single. It was simply part of the all-but-completed debut album whose finishing touches should have occupied the latter part of June. Meanwhile, the Pistols were determined to maintain momentum. In a throwback to the early sixties, when bands issued anywhere up to six singles a year, hardly waiting for one single to go into chart nosedive before dispensing the next dose, the Pistols chose to issue their third 45 and their finest 3 minutes-15 a mere six weeks after "GSTQ" first hit the racks.

The release of "Pretty Vacant" was a masterstroke. The censors were compromised by their own pretense that the Pistols weren't subject to a ban, simply their "offensive" second single. The words of "Pretty Vacant"—save for Rotten making "cant" sound suspiciously like "cunt"—

could hardly ruffle the feathers of even the most prissy peacock. Of course, one listen made it clear that the revolution was most definitely not on hold. *NME*'s anonymous headline summed it up: "ANOTHER SEX PISTOLS RECORD . . . turns out to be the future rock & roll." Roy Carr, taking his brief from our anonymous penman, gave the single its due— hyperbole with the hype an understatement:

> Picture yourself trying to describe the sheer overwhelming impact of "(I Can't Get No) Satisfaction," "My Generation," "Raw Power" or even "Dancing in the Street." Truthfully, there aren't any appro- priate words. And, unless you're terminally insensitive, you can't possibly fail to recognize the numbing shock of reality when, on such rare occasions as these, it presents itself with all the subtlety of an earthquake.
>
> The Sex Pistols' "Pretty Vacant" is one such instance.
>
> With this disc, the Pistols positively cream their closest com- petitors with muscle to spare.
>
> Forget about the acceptable face of outlaw chic. The Sex Pistols are a band virtually unable to perform before a public who helped to create them. It's a vacuum in which no other band has, until now, found itself thrust. As a result of this dilemma, the only posi- tive outlet for their frustrations is the comparative isolation of the recording studio and it's from there that "Pretty Vacant"—the music, the noise, the intense atmosphere—boils over in sheer anger and desperation.
>
> People have been trying to get back to this pitch of intensity throughout the '70s and the cumulative desperation seems finally to erupt on this seminal single.

The final paragraph of *Melody Maker*'s equally laudatory review of "Pretty Vacant" concluded, "This won't need air play to make the chart. If it gets the radio exposure it deserves it will be number one." "God Save the Queen" may have taken a most unorthodox route to the top of the charts, but the release of "Pretty Vacant" showed a band prepared to attack on all fronts: including "Top of the Pops," the BBC's reviled week- ly half-hour TV diet for teensters and pre-teensters starved of moving images of their pop icons.

With "Pretty Vacant" entering the Top Ten a mere 10 days after being shipped to the retail chains (Smiths, Boots et al.), the BBC decided to allow a prerecorded video of the Pistols miming to "Pretty Vacant" to impinge upon their hallowed Thursday 7 P.M. "Top of the Pops" slot. Six months after their notorious appearance on Bill Grundy's chat show, the tabloids had a field day bemoaning the Pistols' return to the halogen tube—despite the innocuousness of the song's sentiments *and* video. (Rotten even spares more tender sensibilities by hiding his buglike stare under a pair of granny-styled shades.) *The Daily Mirror* of July 14, 1977, reported:

> The BBC decision to put the punk rockers on TV is certain to enrage thousands of parents and other viewers. . . . The new record, "Pretty Vacant," jumped forty places this week to No. 7 in the BBC charts, compiled by the British Market Research Bureau. It contains no four-letter words. Top of the Pops producer Robin Nash said: "I have nothing against new wave groups like the Sex Pistols. I have to make a professional judgement and I recognize that at the moment they have a great following." . . . Labour MP Marcus Lipton said: "I think this is quite deplorable and disgusting. I think the BBC should be ashamed."

The day before the "Top of the Pops" screening, the Pistols wisely took off for less-threatening climes—a two-week Scandinavian tour, the first real opportunity for the post-Matlock band to get back to playing live—though not without a final riposte, should *The Daily Mirror* be believed: "Reporters found them at Heathrow Airport—and before long the four-man group was hurling seats around in a departure room. Almost every question received an obscene reply. . . . In one of the politest moments Johnny Rotten said: 'I ain't interested in talking to fabricated people.'"

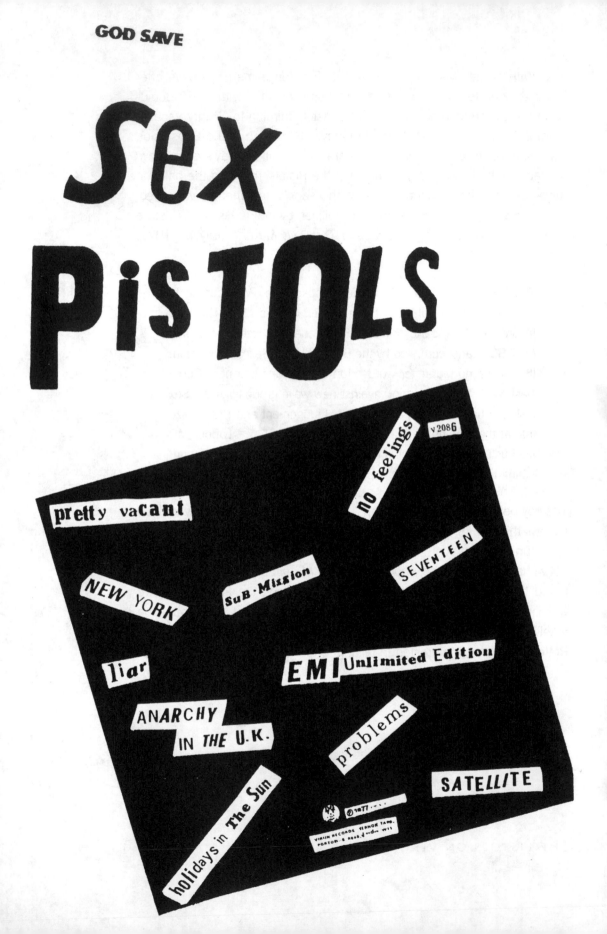

GOD SAVE SEX PISTOLS

And still *God Save Sex Pistols* (the original title for *Bollocks*) stayed absent from Virgin's release schedule. The work in June at Wessex, clearly intended to wrap up the album, did indeed wrap up an album (though not *the* album); the first preview of *Bollocks,* published in late June, suggested that a sequence had now been approved. This "preview," however, did not come in any of the four main music weeklies, or the tabloid dailies, but in a xeroxed, single-staple fanzine with just a few hundred subscribers, by the name of *48 Thrills* (a nod to The Clash song "48 Hours"). The undated review, clearly written before the release of "Pretty Vacant" (the reference to the unreleased status of "No Fun" being the giveaway), runs thus:

> ". . . it's my choice . . . what I want to do . . ."
> Sex Pistols vinyl: totally devastating.
> No doubt that "God Save the Queen" is a great single. On "Anarchy" the sound was a bit off the mark, but this finally captured the excitement on record. The Pistols' song is glorious enough itself to be an anthem, right down to Paul Cook's military drum roll at the end.
> Their sound is now unique; a simple, solid rhythm section—and that's what you dance to!—over which comes Steve Jones's crisp, crackling guitar and the perfect economic solo at the end. Everything crammed magnificently into three minutes.
> The first time they played ["God Save the Queen"], at a gig in Hendon before the Anarchy tour, Rotten told the audience that

he'd only written it that week and he sang the lyrics from a sheet of paper. Not great lyrics, but enough to get up most people's noses.

Everything that the single finally proved about how superb the Sex Pistols actually are will be confirmed when the album comes out. I heard the tape once and it was enough to convince me.

Somehow, Rotten's been captured at his obnoxious best—full of rage, cynicism and humour &c. And, as on the single, the band are in absolute control. The fact that Steve Jones and Paul Cook have been playing together for years shows in the tightness and power of the music. Steve Jones is never too ambitious—many of his slashed riffs are similar, but they create a great wall of wild noise, laden with the usual feedback. All this over the heavy thump of Cook's drumming and the solid basswork (Sid, with a couple of tracks that feature Glen Matlock, and maybe even a bit of Steve Jones's bass).

Most of the tracks on the album are produced by Bill Smith [sic], who used to work with Mott, with a couple—"Anarchy" and "Pretty Vacant"—done by Chris Thomas, who produced the [new] single. The production is great, with none of the murkiness that ruins most of the new wave records we've had so far. Some of the music is chaotic, but everything is crisp and clear.

"Seventeen" is an old favorite from last year. When Rotten first sang it, it wasn't the fashion. It was real and still is now. Shows up all the unimaginative, derivative rubbish for what it is: "On my face not a trace / of reality / We don't care about long hair / We don't wear flaaares! / I'm a lazy sod / I'm a lazy Sid / I'm a lazy sod."

"New York" is another great noisy pop song. Then there's the incredible solo guitar intro. to "Pretty Vacant." It's a bit like the riff that The Clash later used on "I'm So Bored."

The newest song on the album is the Berlin Wall–inspired "Holidays in the Sun," complete with some weird backing vocals.

The only other song on the album that wasn't part of the set at the 100 Club is "EMI"—if anyone has a right to be singing about record companies, it's the group who have been totally uncompromising in their dealings with them.

There's no let up as they speed through versions of "Liar" and "Problems." The remix of "Anarchy in the UK" has the vocals more upfront and sounds slightly slower, but apart from that is no different from the original.

It's followed by the earthy "Submission," a real killer.

"No Feelings" was originally going to be the B-side of the Pistols' A&M single. Lyrically, it's in a class of its own—"I got no emotions for anybody else/You better understand I'm in love with myself/No feelings for anybody else."

"Satellite" has some great lines about suburban life, a riff similar to "Anarchy" and a catchy "I love you" hookline in the chorus.

The album ends with Rotten repeating the word "problem" in a never-ending deadpan tone. That's it—no non-originals. . . . Not even "No Fun," the Stooges number they kept in their live set after kicking out all the other oldies like "Substitute" and "Stepping Stone." I hope that they at least release "No Fun" sometime.

"Actually we're not into music, we're into chaos."

That's what one of the Pistols said in Neil Spencer's first ever review of the group last February.

It's musical chaos, if anything, and it's devastating, superb and danceable.

I'm not saying it can't be bettered, but at the moment it cuts practically everything else to shreds.

So the original album lineup was: "Seventeen," "New York," "Pretty Vacant," "Holidays in the Sun," "EMI," "Liar," "Problems," "Anarchy in the UK," "Submission," "No Feelings," and "Satellite"—eleven songs, two singles. Rotten had always insisted that there would be no non-originals on the album, "just our own, far-out, brilliant stuff," but then he had also insisted that the singles (all save the deleted "Anarchy") would not be on either: "How many LPs have you bought with five tracks released as singles?" he asked Kris Needs in June. Even the Virgin ads for "God Save the Queen" that had previously bedecked the weeklies' back pages proclaimed, "It won't be on the new album and it may not be out at all for very long."

The problem was, the Pistols hadn't recorded any new originals save "Holidays," and if the Pistols were going to be true to their word—no covers, no "God Save the Queen"—then they needed another song (or, preferably, two). The only other preview of *God Save Sex Pistols,* published six weeks later in the more populist *Record Mirror,* reviewed much the same potential artifact. Although "Satellite" remained, "Pretty Vacant" was due for replacement—but with what?

Reporter Travis McGeestrom's idea of insight into the developing album in *Record Mirror* on August 13, 1977, ran as follows:

The beginning is a two-second "Ugh!"; a deep studio grunt leading into "17" (aka "I'm A Lazy Sod"). The well-known anthem gets the full treatment; guitar punching up front, controlled vocal agression from Rotten and an echoed chorus slipping in the odd "I'm a lazy Sid . . ." Just for a start it's got the live power that doesn't falter once—real through romance. But "Pretty Vacant" (originally next in line) is the space to watch. Another track—presently being recorded—will appear on the album since this has already been released as a single.

Then "New York." Guitar thrash and staccato vocals punctuated with the demoniacal laughter/asides that Johnny Rotten excels in give this a punishing two-minute climax, leading into "Holidays in the Sun." Economic, and strongly traditional, riffs carry the Rotten rant here—Rock & roll and an insurgent speed rap that hits the end before it's begun. Again.

And "Liar" takes over with the Pistols in full stride. With the strident chorus of "lie, lie, lie, liar" the melody comes across fast and strong; a shouted, goading hook of "you're in suspension" adds to the tuneful turmoil, giving the song all the frothing urgency it needs. "Problems"—again, old and famous already—takes the first side out. A resonant and echoey vocal rides the backing thump and thrust to build repeatedly to the cutting taunt: "the problem is you . . . and watcha gonna do?" Dance? The flail-out is a crushing, mantralike repetition of "problems." Fade and end.

Side the second (for the moment at least) is kicked off with "Anarchy in the UK," a spot-the-difference job to compare with the EMI mix, and a welcome chance to get the single-that-started-it-all for those who got stopped in their tracks by the ban last year. "Anarchy" is followed by another established song, "Submission." Someone will call this the ballad of the album. Certainly it's a slower brain-punch than the others—an instrumental back-up, reminiscent (even) of Blue Oyster Cult, grinds relentlessly over a chillingly distant vocal and wailing "effects." Effective it is, and this, the longest track by far, ends with sustained vocal and a distant, distinctive Rotten splutter.

You're whacked out of lobotomy immediately with the chopped-chord adrenalin of "No Feelings." One of the most perfect "songs" here, it's again got all the raw power and savage, sardonic exhortation that, simply, is both the invention—and prerogative—of one J. Rotten. For 1977 or any other time.

"Satellite" keeps the pace up. The sarcastic lyrics lead into an incredible "and . . . I love you" chorus that is a dead ringer (and perhaps a loving one) for the Gary Glitter battle cries of old. Really. The massed singing ranks trade off a crazed and frantic lead—ending with a wry pseudowail of "nobody loves me" and doglike yelps.

So to the killer. For last, blast and knockin' out the past. "EMI." This one's unbelievable and here it is. The song about the company. "I tell you it was all a frame/they only did it for the fame/WHO?," Rotten opines, before whining the chorus "EMI . . . EMI . . . EMI." Sarcastic, angry and snarling the power of this song defies description. It runs through three gut-churning riffs with every throwaway, every lip-curl and every bit of spitting fury included. The massed ranks join the end: "And blind acceptance is a sign / Of stupid folk telling lies [sic]/ LIKE/EMI . . . EMI." [Note: The line is actually "of stupid fools who stand in line."] The rasping, croaked conclusion of "EMI . . . goodbye . . . A&M." And the "problem" mantra returns.

Evidently, McGeestrom had heard the same tape as the editor of *48 Thrills* (save for the latter's transposing of "EMI" from track 11 to track 5, making for a seven-song side, surely an error on *48 Thrills'* part) but with the promise of a new track to replace the now-released "Vacant." Interestingly, both reviewers refer to a coda, "the 'Problems' mantra," being taken from the end of side one and replicated at the end of the album. Though no such mantra appears on the final album, "Problems" retained its position at the end of side one, and "EMI" remained at album's end. The idea had an obvious precedent, and a worrying one at that: the reprise at the end of *Sergeant Pepper's Lonely Hearts Club Band,* the final bit of stuffing in that particular turkey.

BOLLOCKS:
THE FINAL SEQUENCE

In fact, the Pistols had returned from Scandinavia with a new song to record. Thomas was recalled to make one final assault on the album he had been working on for nine months, on and off. The song was a dark tale of obsession, blasted through with an existential distaste for the animal in us all. "Bodies" also carried a solid-gold guarantee of no airplay in its determination to break the world record (previously held by Henry Miller?) for f-words in a single sentence, "Fuck this and fuck that, and fuck it all, and fuck the fucking brat."

CHRIS THOMAS: *"Bodies" was great. We sort of changed that around and elevated it. By then I was there for the duration and they brought in one more song and that was "Bodies." It was hardly written. 'Cause John wrote the lyric in first person and third person, in the first person as her singing it, "I don't want a baby like that," and the third person, we did about two or three vocal takes. One was in first person and one was in third, and I always edit between takes. He'd told me about this mad girl who lived in a tree and had accused him of making her pregnant and he was a bit fazed by this whole thing but this song came out of this, and because of what he'd told me when I was doing the "comp." [i.e., editing between vocal takes] on the vocal, because we'd got this thing where it's first person or third person, I implicated him. I expected this bottle to come flying from the back of the control*

92

room but he said, "No, I like that, that's alright," and it stayed like that.

Although the full quartet had allegedly shared in the creation of "Holidays," Jones once again picked up the bass in the studio. However, Sid Vicious made his one audible contribution to *Bollocks* on "Bodies," though "audible" might be overstating the case given the "Panzer division" of guitars that the Jones camp once again called on. Thomas knew better than to wack Vicious up in the mix.

> JOHNNY ROTTON: *Sid was so bad in the studio that even Chris Thomas knew. The whole thing went way over his head so Sid drowned himself in vodka. He could not hold a tune, and I think it was a fear of the whole situation. It was all too much, which is understandable. Sid was thrown into the deep end.*

According to Rotten, in his autobiography, Vicious did make one more contribution to the *Bollocks* sessions, a version of "Submission" that did not make the album.

> JOHNNY ROTTON: *We did some different versions of songs, I did a different version of "Submission" with Sid, which wasn't put on the album. . . . It was a lot different from the Glen Matlock version because it was a hell of a lot less musical and I thought more chaotic and important.*

The version actually on *Bollocks* (originally omitted from the UK album but reinstated when Branson realized it would be available on the French version) hardly sounds unmusical *or* chaotic. Rotten seems to be referring to the version finally released in 1996 on *This Is Crap,* which is, indeed, "a hell of a lot less musical . . . [but] more chaotic and important." This alternate "Submission" is one of the all-time great Sex Pistols recordings, a surprising reconnoitre of the ebullient feel of the July 1976 take. The bass playing—three notes, down neck, three notes, up neck, and so on—sounds too clumsy for Matlock or Jones, although it is never allowed to intrude on what is a truly demonic vocal (and Vicious at least doesn't blow the all-important, four-note intro). The silly voices that found their apotheosis on PiL's "Fodderstompf" are well in evidence, as is that staple of all

British comedy, farting noises. But the exuberance of Rotten's delivery never gets countermanded by Jones, who rediscovers the Townshend touch, albeit "under the water," while Cook, beating a triumphal march throughout, gets to cut loose in a pounding finale. The whole performance, dare I say, sounds live in the studio, noises et al. Not an overdub in sight (okay, there's a double-tracked vocal here and there).

When I say that the Pistols or Thomas/Price made the wrong call, it is clear that this "Submission" was not the only cut on the master-reel that could have been a contender. With "Bodies" in the can, it was time to put the album together, once and for all. According to Savage, "The Sex Pistols album was in chaos, with three different versions of every track available. . . . [In the end] on 20 September, Richard Branson spent a long night selecting versions and track listings: he wanted all the hits on the album, although most of Virgin, Glitterbest and the group were against the idea."

There never were three different versions of all 12 *Bollocks* cuts. The Pistols had 13 tracks from which to perm an album, three of which, as of September, had come out as singles, though "Anarchy in the UK" was long deleted and was always going to be on the album. Of the non-single tracks, alternates are known for four of them—"EMI," "Submission," "No Feelings," and "Seventeen." These alternates, along with the original "album" mix of "Satellite," appear on the second volume of *This Is Crap,* without explanation or annotation, sandwiched between the Spedding demos and the Denmark Street "Anarchy in the UK." In fact, all five *Bollocks* alternates originate from a 10-track reel of Wessex takes and rough sold in auction at Sotheby's in London in the late eighties, the full reel comprising:

EMI—take 1 [alternate]
Submission—take 1 [alternate]
Satellite [alternate mix]
No Feelings [alternate]
Seventeen [alternate]
Bodies [*Bollocks*]
New York [*Bollocks*]
Liar [*Bollocks*]
EMI—take 2 [*Bollocks*]
Submission—take 2 [*Bollocks*]

The fact that this tape comprises versions of eight of the tracks to make *Bollocks* and five actual album cuts suggests that this was some kind of master reel, to which potential contenders for album status had at some point been pulled. The copy sold in auction was presumably a "safety," or backup copy of the actual master. The absence of "Problems," the only non-single missing from the reel, may perhaps suggest that this song was not recorded at Wessex. Thomas recalls an attempt to record one or more songs at AIR Studios, Thomas's home-away-from-home, where he had carved out a career with Roxy Music over four albums of almost flawless Britrock. "Problems" is perhaps one that Thomas gave some air.

Since the alternates of "Submission" and "Satellite" both make the grade, sonicwise and chopswise, how well do the other three alternates stand up to their more famed kin? The alternate "EMI" probably contains the superior Rotten vocal but otherwise sounds like little more than a demo, while "No Feelings," though it has its share of clever guitar fills and frills, has a vocal culled from the lackluster department. The alternate "Seventeen," on the other hand, though clearly an experiment, has much to recommend it. Taking an almost Goodmanesque approach to one of their hoariest ditties, a buzzsaw guitar distorted-to-fuzz hogs the right speaker, while Rotten, imagining himself on the Highbury terraces, remains resolutely left field, lazing on a Saturday afternoon: "I'm so layzzee." Though it has none of the hey-ho-let's-go immediacy of the *Bollocks* cut, the alternate "Seventeen" suggests a happy middle ground between the Goodman and Thomas methods and was perhaps one of Price's attempts at trying something different for its own sake.

That the Pistols reached September 20 without finalizing a sequence for *Bollocks* suggests how bogged down by the process they had become. A secret tour of the UK at the tail-end of August, billed as the SPOTS (Sex Pistols On Tour Secretly), had delayed things once more. It was almost as if the band were scared to let go of its one remaining commodity: its 1976 repertoire. The delay was such that McLaren and the band agreed that a fourth single was in order, a miscalculation that would put the first chink in the Pistols' public amour.

The decision to release a fourth single turned *Bollocks* from a long-awaited debut album into a greatest hits collection. Required to utilize two of the 13 tracks scheduled for the album—"Holidays in the Sun" b/w "Satellite"—the Pistols left themselves just 11 tracks to perm an album from, including all three singles to date. Perhaps at one point they were considering "Submission" as single number 4—hence its omission from the first UK pressing of *Bollocks.* The first 10,000 copies came as an 11-track album, with a quite different sequence (see discography) and a single-sided 45 of "Submission," slipped in at the last minute. However, by the beginning of October, it was clear that the next 45 would be "Holidays" and that all *four* A-sides would be on the album, including "God Save the Queen" (thus ensuring that the LP would not be stocked by Boots, Woolworth's, and W. H. Smith).

Evidently, Rotten at least wanted to make a statement by issuing one of the new songs as a single and, since "Bodies" had even less chance of airplay than "God Save the Queen," "Holidays" it was. Rotten had told an English journalist on the Swedish tour, back in July, that "Holidays" would probably be the next single; evidently, the idea had been allowed a period of gestation. Unfortunately, "Holidays" was in for a rough ride. Though awarded the ubiquitous Single of the Week by both *Sounds* and *Melody Maker,* both papers took potshots at the similarity of the single to other recent punk offerings.

Melody Maker gave the Pistols the benefit of the doubt: "Don't be misled into thinking that Chris Thomas might just as easily have taken bits from 'Vacant' and 'Did You No Wrong' and then remixed them. The similarities are there but that's how Les Pistolets SOUND."

Sounds did not: "You can't tell me that they don't know they're ripping off the Jam's 'In The City' riff. I like the Pistols so much that I'd love to believe that it was a completely unconscious lift, but even if it was, the very first person they played it to would surely have pointed it out to them."

In *NME* the reviewer was crueler still, with a headline of "No Chewn, My Babe, No Chewn" and a putdown par excellence/plea for the return of some pop sensibilities:

> And the triumphant path blazed by "Anarchy in the UK," "God
> Save the Queen" and "Pretty Vacant" begins to falter. "Holidays
> in the Sun"—the first Pistols A-side composed by Jones/Cook
> /Rotten/Vicious as opposed to Jones/Cook/Rotten/Matlock—has
> two out of the three elements that have graced the classic triad
> of hits: it has great lyrics and a wild-eyed mean-machine of a riff,
> but it lacks the structure and immediacy that was, presumably,

the contribution of the more pop-oriented Glen Matlock. The result is a shapeless rant rather than a song. . . . The other singles were great POP as well as great rock and roll—plus I thought formless self-indulgence was a BOF failing. Tighten up, star.

Worse was to come. If the Pistols' songs had always courted the offensive, their sleeves had not. Even "God Save the Queen" had not been released with the safety-pinned Liz that graced posters and T-shirts. Virgin, however, was shown a glimpse of the shape of things to come when, five days after the release of "Holidays," the Belgian Travel Service sought an injunction claiming copyright infringment for the images daubed on the single's picture sleeve. It was purloined from one of their brochures by Reid, presumably unaware that anonymous Gallic artists aren't quite as bound by copyright laws as paid record-sleeve designers. As a result, 60,000 sleeves at Virgin had to be promptly destroyed, and the single temporarily withdrawn, quickly re-released in a plain white sleeve, thus creating yet another Pistols single rarity to put alongside the EMI "Anarchy" and the A&M "Queen."

The single itself was something of a flop, peaking at a disappointing eight (two places below "Vacant"), and remaining in the top 20 for just four weeks. Its popularity was doubtless curtailed in part by an announcement the day the picture sleeve was withdrawn (October 20) that the Pistols' debut album would follow on November 4 and, despite previous assurances, would indeed open with the new single, "Holidays in the Sun."

Virgin, in a desperate attempt to deflect flak for the inclusion of the singles, let it be known that there was "a strong possibility of an alternative album being issued at about the same time on which two of their former hit singles . . . would be replaced by two new tracks, plus a new LP title." According to the spokesman presenting this whimsical idea, "We've put the singles on the LP because most people wanted it that way. But the alternative set would enable us to overcome the multiple stores' ban." This particular foggy notion got as far as a test pressing, though, needless to say, minus any "two new tracks." "Submission" and "Satellite" seem to have been the intended "bonus tracks" at a time when *Bollocks* was scheduled to be an 11-track album. The "alternate" 10-track test pressing included:

Side 1: "Body" (apparently the original title), "New York," "Submission," "Liar," "EMI"

Side 2: "Problems," "No Feelings," "Seventeen," "Sattelite" [*sic*] and "Anarchy." (The notion of two versions of an album, one with singles and one without, was appropriated by stiff artist Wreckless Eric who, the following month, issued his debut album in 12" jet-black and 10" shit-brown formats, with and without "Whole Wide World" and "Telephoning Home.")

Meanwhile, *Never Mind the Bollocks, Here's the Sex Pistols* had not even made it out of the warehouse when Branson found that he had two Sex Pistols albums contending with his. After a year without any Pistols long-players, fans suddenly found themselves with a dazzling array of options.

The decision to nix the "alternative" album option was certainly made after the press release of October 20, which gave just 11 tracks for *Bollocks.* The French had apparently already added 'Submission' to the original 11-track album. Rather than resequencing, they had put "Submission" after "Problems," i.e., at the end of side one, thus lousing up the Pistols' intended sequence. Ominously for Branson, the French were planning to release their version a week ahead of Virgin.

Since McLaren had negotiated the French deal with Barclay Records separately from, indeed prior to, the Virgin deal, there was nothing Branson could do to halt the French presses. As a man previously convicted for VAT avoidance on "exported" copies of albums, Branson was fully aware how easy it was to bring European copies of vinyl into Britain—whatever his contract with the Pistols said. To compound Branson's fast-growing headache, the Pistols had not only made the last-minute decision to include "Submission" but wished to resequence the album, with both new songs now opening the sonic fare.

Although Branson managed to put his plant in overdrive mode in order to move the album's release forward a week, French copies were still on the boulevards of Britain first. Ten thousand 11-track albums (all with "bonus" single) compounded the initial confusion. A few thousand copies with 11 tracks listed on the sleeve but 12 tracks on the record gave some further fans false hope of a collectors' item. The 11-track *Bollocks* remains highly collectible, largely because of its novelty value, but also because the alternate sequence makes for a quite different listening experience.

If the multiple versions of *Bollocks* were intended to further the cause of Anarchy, then McLaren had once again proved a master tactician. Not only had he forced Virgin to pull out all the stops just to get the album out, but he had also made them abide by the band's last-minute decision to include "Submission" by giving Barclay the track too. (In normal circumstances, Virgin might just have refused—but not now; fans would have simply bought the 12-track French version.) He had also generally fucked with "the hippies." (McLaren never stopped viewing Virgin as a bunch of would-be hippies.)

But the French *Bollocks* was not the only item competing for fans' denarii, and, once again, it was McLaren who was suspected of doing the dirty on Virgin. It has always been a mystery how a bootlegger got his hands on pristine tapes of the July 1976 demos, the Goodman "Anarchy," and the January 1977 Gooseberry sessions. Nonetheless, these studio tapes appeared as an album called *Spunk* on a label called Blank in early October 1977. Some pointed the finger at Goodman (and even at the disgruntled Matlock), but most waggled it in the direction of that self-styled stunt-puller Mr. McLaren. Apart from anything, McLaren had never made a secret of the fact that he considered the Goodman tapes to be the "real" Pistols. Savage's *England's Dreaming* strongly implies that McLaren knew all along how *Spunk* came out at the very point when Virgin were hoping for a *Bollocks* bonanza:

> Right up to the moment of rush release [of *Bollocks*], on 28th October, rows were going on between the group and Virgin about what should go on the album. Glitterbest took advantage of the confusion to insert some confusion of their own. In late October, a Sex Pistols bootleg entitled *No Future UK* [*sic*] was released under the fictional group name of *Spunk*. These were recordings made from the Goodman tapes . . . which McLaren preferred to the finished album. . . . [Although] Glitterbest owned the tapes—as they had paid for both recordings outside any contract—the release was in breach of the Virgin deal.

In his account Savage has confused two bootlegs, *No Future UK* and *Spunk*. *Spunk* was the 12-track bootleg album that appeared beneath certain record counters the week before *Bollocks*. *No Future UK* was a 15-track album, incorporating all of *Spunk,* as well as the full, seven-minute "No Fun" and alternates of "Pretty Vacant" and "Anarchy," which did not appear in the seedier London markets until the early months of 1979.

SPUNK AND THE
ART OF CHAOS

It was *Sounds* that broke the story of *Spunk*'s existence in a two-page story in its October 22, 1977, issue, and it was Chas De Whalley who first imbued the Goodman tapes with the potentially combustible powder of Rocklore. Having been sent to a "Ladbroke Grove grotto" (i.e., the Rough Trade store, soon to become a leading indie label, at this point happy to fund operations with a little less-than-kosher product), De Whalley's copy of *Spunk* came with the matrix number scratched out, but otherwise intact. De Whalley proceeded to inquire of the man who produced the tracks in question, Dave Goodman; the EMI A&R man that had signed and dropped the band, Nick Mobbs; and of the Pistols' office itself, whence these tapes may have come. None was willing to own up. De Whalley, however, couldn't resist hinting at the person he viewed as the obvious culprit: "Seasoned Pistols observers suggested that Malcolm McLaren might have been behind [*Spunk*] (in the interests of Anarchy and Complete Control—dig) but this was firmly denied (in his absence) by his secretary."

De Whalley capped his article with the sort of quote that money can't buy, one pen stroke upping the stakes in the critical battleground that was fast opening up: "All in all, and despite the fact that it's a bootleg and illegal and everything, *Spunk* is an album no self-respecting rock fan would turn his nose up at. I've been playing it constantly for a week, and I'm not bored yet."

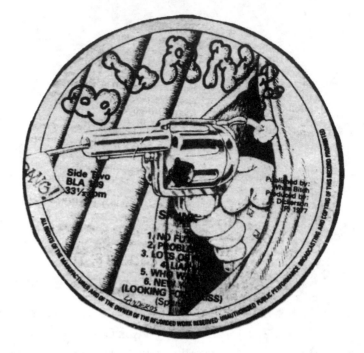

As I wrote in *Bootleg,* "No way could *Spunk* have been the Pistols' legacy to the pop world. But as an alternative 'debut' it was brilliantly conceived. *Never Mind the Bollocks* might have sounded like a good hard-rock album for the seventies, but *Spunk* was just four teenagers locked upstairs in a room in Denmark Street, cutting loose and blowing away the cobwebs of the seventies."

If, as the late great Lester Bangs once wrote, "producers, for the most part, serve absolutely no purpose beyond gussying up something fresh and alive on demos and running the band over and over the same ground till the whole place is a cemetery," then Chris Thomas and Bill Price had done a damn fine job. But to many, fans and critics alike, *Spunk* was the real McCoy. Inevitably, reviews of *Spunk* were tagged to the end of reviews for *Bollocks,* though not all agreed that *Spunk* was the superior artifact. Kris Needs in *ZigZag* chose the minority view: "In most cases the *Bollocks* cuts are superior although the bootleg naturally ain't got such a good sound and the versions of 'Submission' and 'Anarchy' are better, 'specially the latter where John sounds throatier, deranged and homicidal."

Julie Burchill, on the other hand, for once managed to avoid viewing the world arse-end up and, in what might pass for measured tones in the Burchillian universe, suggested: "The singing [on *Spunk*] is done with much less expertise, Rotten sounding sick to death. It's a much better record."

McLaren may have been amused by the presence of *Spunk* in the marketplace—regardless of who exactly had been operating the press— but clearly others in the organization were less enamored of the notion. On a Radio One interview designed to promote *Bollocks,* Rotten and Vicious were asked about the bootleg. Vicious proceeded to complain about "the principle of the matter, some stupid fool with a tape recorder making a million pounds out of some concert where we sweated our guts out," before interviewer John Tobler pointed out that these were studio recordings. (He refrained from mentioning that Vicious did not play a single note on the bootleg.) Rotten, who had stronger grounds for grievance, dismissed the artifact: "[It's] dreadful. All that is material we didn't want released, 'cause to us it's substandard and should be kept unreleased at our discretion not some . . . git's."

THE RECEPTION
AWAITING BOLLOCKS

Regardless of the merits of either album, the punters who were buying *Spunk* (and even to this day *Spunk* probably remains one of the two or three bestselling vinyl bootlegs) were bound also to buy *Bollocks*. What it afforded the UK fan was the opportunity to compare and contrast two distinct phases of development, indeed two quite different bands—a no-star-vehicle Britpop quartet, and a powerhouse trio with bad attitude. Ironically, the to-my-ears slick sound of *Bollocks* was still deemed rough'n'ready by the American critics. Paul Nelson, in his exuberant review in *Rolling Stone,* considered:

> In a commercial sense . . . the Sex Pistols will probably destroy no one but themselves, but theirs is a holy or unholy war that isn't really going to be won or lost by statistics, slick guitar playing or smooth studio work. This band still takes rock & roll personally, as a matter of honour and necessity, and they play with an energy and conviction that is positively transcendent in its madness and fever.

If Nelson and his kind could not see *Bollocks* as a commercial proposition, his British counterparts knew that (at least in the Motherland) it most certainly was. Few debut albums had ever been as eagerly awaited as the UK edition of *Never Mind the Bollocks*—evinced by advance orders of 125,000, more than enough to send *Bollocks* to the number one slot on the album charts the week after its release—and even fewer debut

105

albums have emerged into the light with so few of its potential purchasers familiar with the contents within, singles excepted. Given that less than 5 percent of those who purchased *Bollocks* that first week had ever seen the band live, it was up to the critics to communicate how much the artifact reflected the band as a live entity—or not.

As it is, the sound of the album stunned even the chosen few. *Spunk* devotees may have commented on the "edge" that the band had "back then," but for stax-o'-guitar-trax, *Bollocks* was the proverbial dog's bollocks [*sic*]. Professional apologists who reviewed the album for the music press donned their most supercilious sneers to pour scorn on the nonbelievers who'd ever doubted that this was one tight rock & roll band (at least when multitracking):

> One of the most brilliant and important sets of lethal rock & roll ever trapped on vinyl. (Chris Brazier, *Melody Maker*)

> None of this [hoopla] would be taken seriously at all if they didn't play classic rock & roll and weren't one of the best and most consistent *recording* bands this year. (Jon Savage, *Sounds*)

> Musically, *Never Mind the Bollocks* is just about the most exciting rock & roll record of the '70s. It's all speed, not nuance . . . and the songs all hit like amphetamines or the plague, depending on your point of view. (Paul Nelson, *Rolling Stone*)

Nelson's comment that *Bollocks* "is all speed" may have sounded like mere confirmation to the uninitiated, whose concept of punk was probably rooted in the cacophonous dentist-drill of The Ramones. Unfortunately, the Pistols were acquiring critical kudos precisely at the point when they were losing their sound live. Even discounting the obvious—that, musically, Vicious was a liability with a large, blood-red "L"—Jones was rapidly becoming just a little too convinced of his own guitar-hero status.

Comparing *Spunk* and *Bollocks,* what really stands out on *Bollocks* is that sense of a band cranked up high. The early Pistols had always preferred the poptones of the Small Faces, early Who, and Kinks as the bedrock for reinventing Britpop. (There is a lovely moment on the June 1976 Free Trade Hall tape when Rotten introduces "Submission" with, "This is a pop song!" and some wag retorts, "Aren't they all?") Indeed,

Matlock recalls in his autobiography, the one time Goodman tried to speed things up:

> Dave was casting around for things to alter [on "Anarchy"]. He—and Malcolm—started trying to get us to play faster and . . . this ran counter to what we considered The Pistols' sound to be about. The Pistols always sounded best when they were playing at a steady, confident pace, not too fast.

In fact, reviewers regularly highlighted "Submission," the song the band had originally intended to omit from *Bollocks* for the contrast it afforded the album:

> "Submission" . . . is my favorite track at the moment. Reminiscent of the early Stooges, it's the only slow number, hypnotic, like a mantric hang-out loosening you up for the final rush. (Brazier, *MM*)

> "Submission" has always been a great track and it's one of the best here, maybe because it's taken at a slower pace than the rest and isn't a million miles away from being dopey. (Jon Savage, *Sounds*)

Both new songs on the album came in for some stick. Chris Brazier, in his *Melody Maker* review, refers to "Holidays"'s "hookless chorus and a complete non-event masquerading as a guitar solo." Listening to something as layered as *Bollocks* certainly required a little patience in order to disentangle the good from the great. If the dense sound could dissuade, it could also end up being attributed with a certain apocalyptic import: "Their music isn't pretty indeed, it often sounds like two subway trains crashing together under forty feet of mud, victims screaming—but it has an Ahab-versus-Moby Dick power" (Paul Nelson, *Rolling Stone*).

Of course, the four singles, cunningly spaced across both sides, operated as a lever for British listeners to find their way into the syrup of sound. As Paul Nelson recognized in his *Rolling Stone* review, "a majority of young Americans are probably going to misunderstand much of the no-survivors, not-even-us stance of the punk-rock/New Wave anarchy in the UK (compared to which, the music of the Ramones sounds like it was invented by Walt Disney)." And yet it was to be in America that the impact of the album would resonate with all the ringing clarity cult status can bestow, taking a generation of miscreants out of the FM/AOR loop. In the UK, *Bollocks* may have made number one in week one, but the Pistols were already being superseded by their spawn. The Only Ones, Magazine, Wire, Siouxsie & the Banshees, Doll By Doll, Joy Division, and Lydon's own PiL would all record albums in the following 18 months that would redefine the form far more radically than *Bollocks*.

With hindsight's granny glasses, it is even possible to see the after-glow of mission accomplished. Jon Savage in an ambiguous final para-graph in *Sounds* noted: "Feel somehow that new songs smack of a creep-ing contrivance . . . and, yeah, what's fine on a single as blast wears me down with nihilism over an album."

But perhaps it was a damn Yankee who displayed the greatest fore-sight of all. Toby Goldstein's album review in *Crawdaddy* suggested that *Bollocks* may just turn out to be the summation of a career, not a promise of songs to come. In his final paragraph, Goldstein confidently assumed the mantle of modern-day prophet:

> ["Bodies"]—brimful with fucks—is one of two numbers written with Sid Vicious instead of former bassist Glen Matlock. It raises a hard question [about] the Pistols' future. . . . It would be a tremen-dous shame if Matlock, who split with the band because he want-ed more melody, was proven to be the control factor behind their high-tension, snowballing, first-rate rock & roll gift, while what remains behind is unchanneled rage. Johnny Rotten is far too charismatic a figure to risk self-parody. But faced with the accusa-tion, he'd probably let fly a huge gob and sneer he don't care.

BOLLOCKS ON TRIAL

The combination of "Bodies"—full to the brim, indeed, with the f-word—the sacrilegious "God Save the Queen," and an album title straight out of Chaucer had not silenced the band's roar. The inevitable ban by the large retail chains only turned the album into an even greater bonanza than "GSTQ" for the independent outlets. *The Sun* had tried to whip up another "'four-letter' storm" in a teacup on the day of the album's release, focusing on the "filthy" "Bodies" and garnering a couple of bite-size quotes from the Tory shadow education minister Norman St. John Stevas. "Bodies" was apparently "the kind of music that is a symptom of the way society is declining. It could have a shocking effect on young people," while the album containing the song had clearly "been produced deliberately to offend."

Once again, *The Sun* was merely generating the kind of publicity money can't buy. Teenagers the country over were delighted to have a further opportunity of cocking two Agincourt archers' fingers at the sanctimonious tabloids. Silencing the Pistols had become the primary preoccupation of the nation's society for small minds. In 1967 the society had almost succeeded in incarcerating The Rolling Stones' frontman, Mick Jagger, before William Rees-Moog, in his famous editorial in *The Times*, asked his loaded question, "Who breaks a butterfly on a wheel?" (The most innocuous of drug convictions was quashed on appeal.) The question they wanted the answer to 10 years on: "Do we get to win this time?"

The forces of darkness seemed to be massing. At the end of October, Capital Radio banned "Holidays in the Sun," though only after it

THE Sun

Friday, November 25, 1977   6p   **TODAY'S TV: PAGES 14 and 15**

TODAY'S TV: PAGES 14 and 15

'TRIAD BOSS' HELD

By ROBERT TRAINI

SCOTLAND YARD have arrested a Chinese restaurant proprietor who is believed to be a top Triad boss.

Detectives are trying to smash two Triads — Chinese secret societies — which are operating in many parts of Britain.

And they described the arrest as a major breakthrough in their fight against protection rackets, blackmail, heroin-smuggling and other major crimes.

The man was arrested in Newport, Gwent, yesterday morning.

Arrests

He was taken to London where he joined three other Chinese who have been held at Harrow Road Police Station, Paddington, since Monday.

Several other Chinese are already before courts on a variety of charges.

All the arrests have followed undercover operations by a special Scotland Yard anti-Triad squad led by Det Chief Supt Fred Luff.

Last night he was interviewing the four men at Harrow Road and charges were expected later.

AND THE SAME TO YOU!

Sex Pistols shoot down

'Colonel Bogey' protest

NEVER MIND . . . Christopher Seale yesterday with the controversial record cover

THE EIGHT - LETTER word immortalised by troops as they marched to the tune of Colonel Bogey is not indecent, magistrates reluctantly decided yesterday.

That gives punk rocker Johnny Rotten and his foul - mouthed Sex Pistols the chance to put up two fingers to the world and say: "And the same to you!"

And it means that thousands of record sleeves with the word

By BRIAN DIXON

on them can go on display.

Record shop manager Christopher Seale was cleared of four charges, under an 88-year-old law, of displaying indecent printed matter in his store in King Street, Nottingham.

VULGAR

Magistrates at Nottingham heard that a policewoman removed two record sleeves of the groups' new LP — Never Mind The Bollocks . . . Here's The Sex Pistols — from Seale's shop window.

Bus inspector Charles Whit-

bread complained to police when he spotted more of the sleeves two days later.

Magistrates' chairman Mr Douglas Betts told 25-year-old Seale: "Much as we deplore the vulgar exploitation of the worst instincts of human nature for commercial profit, we must reluctantly find you not guilty."

Similar charges were dropped against Richard Branson, whose Virgin Records company produced the record and sell it in their 350 shops.

Mr Betts and two women colleagues on the bench were given the origins and definitions of the word by university professor James Kinsley.

Professor Kinsley, an Anglican priest and head of the English Department at Nottingham University said the word appeared in almost every language in one form or another.

STONES

He told the court that the word was common in Scandinavian and Germanic languages and meant a small ball.

It appeared in medieval Bibles but had been changed to stones by later translators.

In the 19th Century, said the Professor, the word had become vulgar —but that did not mean rude. It meant it had become popular and was used colloquially.

And he added: " It meant and means that

Continued on Page Two

If they're in the news, they're in The Sun

LOVERS IN A WORLD OF THEIR OWN

PAGE 5

Bolan's girl may face crash charge

PAGE 11

GOODIES GET THE ROYAL HEAVE-HO

PAGE 7

PAGE 5
PAGE 11
PAGE 7

had entered the Capital charts. Someone, somewhere up there, had listened to the record and decided that in singing the line, "I don't wanna go to the new Belsen," Rotten was likening Belsen to a holiday camp (Huh?). By November 4, advertising the album on commercial radio had gone the way of all flesh, while even in the music press *Record Mirror* had run a full-page ad for *Bollocks,* but with the *Record Mirror* logo slapped across the word *Bollocks.* The IBA (Independent Broadcasting Authority) endorsed a ban on adverts for the album implemented by the Association of Independent Radio Contractors. The album title was the ostensible cause of offense. However, at least one voice instrumental in the blanket ban was prepared to come clean about the association's true motives and the true target of their censorious acts: the product itself. John Jackson, spokesman for the Independent Television Companies Association, in explaining their refusal of a £40,000 TV ad campaign planned by Virgin, revealed that:

> "[It was] not the wording of the forms of the ads but the product itself we object to. The decision was unanimous. But this is not a ban for all time. If there is another Pistols album, we would consider it on its merits."

Even the Pistols' old label, EMI, seemed keen to join in the fun. Rather than letting sleeping dogs tell the truth, the Group Trade Mark Executive of EMI Limited, one D.C.C. Pick, sent a registered letter containing an unequivocal threat to the managing director of Virgin Records Limited (i.e., Richard Branson). The formal letter, dated November 2, read thus:

> Dear Sir,
>   Our attention has been drawn to a record issued recently for sale by your company by the "Sex Pistols" under reference number V2086. You have used the letters "EMI" on the reverse side of the outer sleeve in which the record is contained and on the label for Side Two of that record.
>   As you are aware, EMI Limited is the proprietor in the United Kingdom of Trade Marks which consist of the letters "EMI" and Marks of which those letters form a substantial part. . . . [Our] Trade Mark registrations cover the use of the letters "EMI" on or in connection with, "inter alia," records and tapes. Your use of "EMI"

on the cover and label of the above-mentioned record appears to constitute an infringement of our rights in these Trade Marks under the Trade Marks Act, 1938.

Having hereby notified you of the ownership of the "EMI" Trade Marks, we wish to reserve our rights to take whatever action we may consider to be necessary for the further protection of our Trade Marks, whether in respect of the above-mentioned record or any other record which may be issued by you.

This was not the only legal storm on the horizon. The album was still at number one, despite (and, in part, because of) the blatant acts of censorship exercised by media and retail outlets alike. The Metropolitan police decided to visit all of the capital's Virgin branches and inform them that they faced prosecution under the 1899 Indecent Advertisements Act if they continued to maintain their window displays for *Never Mind the Bollocks,* that is, poster-sized copies of the album cover. Although displays were removed or "toned down," the police seemed bent on suppressing the artifact itself. On November 9, the front-page headline of the *London Evening Standard* read, "Police Move in on Punk Disc Shops":

A record-shop manager was arrested this afternoon in connection with the display of a controversial new punk rock disc by The Sex Pistols. The record—entitled *Never Mind the Bollocks, Here's The Sex Pistols*—is already at number one in some charts [*sic*], and earned the group a gold disc. Police have warned a number of record shops around the country, including London, that they risk prosecution if they prominently display the record.

The man arrested is Mr Chris Seal [*sic*], manager of the Virgin Records shop in King Street, Nottingham. Nottinghamshire police said that he was likely to be appearing in court later this afternoon or tomorrow. In London, record shop manager Mr Pete Sennett has been warned by the police to cover up the word "bollocks." Mr Sennett, manager of Small Wonder Records in Walthamstow, said: "A policeman came into the shop and told me I'd be prosecuted if I didn't take the sleeve out of the window or cover up the word bollocks. I must say it's a bit Victorian but we have now covered the word up."

> Virgin Records, which records The Sex Pistols music, said: "We've had reports that several shops have been visited by the police in the last few days. The objection is based on the title and not any illustration."

Seale, it would appear, willingly set himself up as a target, possibly at Branson's behest. Constantly challenging police authority, he had been warned on four separate occasions between November 5—when police-person Ms. Storey had first seen the album sleeve "with the word bollocks not obscured in any way" (oh me, oh my)—and November 9, when Seale was arrested, that he might face prosecution under the Indecent Advertising Act of 1889. He continued to display copies of the album and its attendant poster in the window of the Nottingham branch of Virgin. Indeed, after all four visits, he promptly replaced displays as soon as the police had departed. Branson was quick to announce that Virgin would meet all of employee Seale's legal costs, and he retained the highly eminent QC John Mortimer, author of the famous *Rumpole of the Bailey* series, to defend Virgin's interests. Branson himself had been prosecuted under this anachronistic piece of legal driftwood back in 1970 (for a leaflet produced for the Student Advisory Centre), the first occasion he had had recourse to Mr. Mortimer's services. It was to prove a wise choice.

Meanwhile, advertisements in the following week's music papers were clearly designed to politicize the issue—and hopefully generate even more sales for the hit album. Beneath a full-page montage of press cuttings with headlines like "Sex Pistols in a new 'Four Letter' Storm," "Police Swoop," "New Sex Pistols Record Banned," and "Pistols Film Shocker" lay a simple message: "THE ALBUM WILL LAST. THE SLEEVE MAY NOT."

The case itself was due to be heard at Nottingham Magistrates Court on November 24. A trial by magistrates gave the Crown Prosecution Service the best chance of success. Magistrates were (and are) almost entirely untrained in the subtleties of jurisprudence, being simply members of the public with too much time on their hands (usually fiftysomething and waiting to roll up the carpet), with only the most simplistic of outlooks when it came to issues like free speech, indeed any fundamental civil rights. Meanwhile, independent retail outlets kept the dayglo sleeves to *Bollocks* inside their shops, wondering if this intrinsically absurd test case might yet decide the fate of the Pistols' album.

Mortimer was determined to present the case as a simple matter of discrimination by the police against four free-thinking teenage spokesmen. Cross-examining the arresting officer, he asked why the *Evening Standard* and the *Guardian* had not been charged under the same act for referring to the album by its full title in stories on the controversy (and, in the *Guardian*'s case, for reproducing the offending cover). When the magistrate overseeing the case asked what point Mortimer was trying to make, he explained he was trying to establish the motives behind the police prosecution. It appeared to Mortimer (and anyone else with synapses at something approaching optimum output) that here was an obvious case of double standards operating to the detriment of his clients; that is, "bollocks" was only indecent when it appeared on a Sex Pistols album.

The prosecutor, Mr. Ritchie, called this an "astonishing suggestion," before proceeding to conduct his cross-examination as if the album itself, and not its lurid visage, was on trial for indecency. *Sounds* journalist Caroline Coon was repeatedly questioned about the use of the word "fuck" on "a song on the album" but professed not to know what Ritchie was talking about. Ritchie's attempt to juxtapose the word "fuck," as it appeared on the album, and the word "bollocks," as it appeared on the cover, failed when he was unable to cite the relevant song ("Bodies") or the relevant lines (lines that may well have antagonized the magistrates sitting astride the bench).

Ritchie made a further attempt to place "bollocks" in the same box as more familiar four-letter words of ill-repute during his cross-examination of Mortimer's expert, and "star," witness, Professor James Kingsley, head of English at the local university. Kingsley had convincingly shown that "bollocks" (or, more accurately, "ballocks") had appeared in written records from the year 1000 and that it had even appeared in place names, much like Maidenhead (he wisely refrained from citing the somewhat more graphic examples like Gropecunt Lane), as well as being deemed an appropriate word by such literary luminaries as Shakespeare, Dylan Thomas, and James Joyce. Kingsley also helpfully explained that:

> The word has been used as a nickname for clergymen. Clergymen
> are known to talk a great deal of rubbish, and so the word later

developed the meaning of nonsense. They became known for talking a great deal of bollocks, just as "old balls" or "baloney" also comes to mean testicles, so it has its twin uses in the dictionary. I would take the album title to mean "Never Mind The Nonsense, Here's The Sex Pistols."

At this point, Mr. Ritchie, stymied by the witness's obvious credentials and grasp of language, once again tried to derail the argument by asking whether, since Professor Kingsley had quoted from *The Dictionary of Slang,* the book in question also contained the words "fuck," "cunt," and "shit." Professor Kingsley's reply once again denied Mr. Ritchie the opportunity to depart from a pertinent avenue of questioning: "If the word fuck does not appear in the dictionary, it should."

If Ritchie's summation merely reiterated his brief, Mortimer's summation firmly nailed the Pistols' album cover to the mast of free speech, and slyly asked the magistrates to consider why exactly this case was being brought:

> One wonders what the world is to think about a judicial system which has to spend its time to consider a word that is used to describe a load of nonsense, balderdash. . . . One wonders why a word which had been dignified by writers from the Middle Ages, in the translation of the Bible, to the works of George Orwell and Dylan Thomas, and which you may find in the dictionary, should be singled out as criminal because it is on a record sleeve by The Sex Pistols. It was because it was The Sex Pistols and not Donald Duck or Katherine Ferrier that this prosecution has been brought.

It took the magistrates just twenty minutes to recognize their civic duty, though the chief pontificator couldn't resist sticking in his thrupenny-worth as the facade of impartiality finally slipped, and his words fell to the floor:

> Much as my colleagues and I wholeheartedly deplore the vulgar exploitation of the worst instincts of human nature for the purchase of commercial profits by both you [Seale] and your company, we must *reluctantly* find you not guilty on each of the four charges.

As the press gathered outside, Johnny Rotten, the one attendant Pistol, cried, "Bollocks is legal. Bollocks! Bollocks! Bollocks!" The following day's *Sun* even carried a front-page shot of Mr. Seale proudly displaying "the controversial record cover" and one of those timeless *Sun* headlines: AND THE SAME TO YOU!:

> The eight-letter word immortalised by troops as they marched to the tune of Colonel Bogey is not indecent, magistrates reluctantly decided yesterday. That gives punk rocker Johnny Rotten and the foul-mouthed Sex Pistols the chance to put up two fingers to the world and say: "And the same to you!" And it means that thousands of record sleeves with the word on them can go [back] on display.

The *Bollocks* saga was over. The Pistols themselves had less than two months left in them. Courting controversy had overtaken music making as their primary preoccupation. In the wee hours of the morning after the Nottingham verdict, Rotten was still quaffing champagne, discussing the next Sex Pistols single with an *NME* journalist. "Belsen Was a Gas" was in a long line of provocative statements by the band. The difference was that "Belsen Was a Gas" was genuinely in poor taste. *The Sun,* for once, expressed the feelings of both punks and parents in their December 1977 editorial: "The Sex Pistols' latest 'song'—heaven help us—is called 'Belsen Was a Gas.' If they don't know why this is highly offensive to millions of people, then they really ARE sick."

Debuted in Holland at the beginning of December, "Belsen Was a Gas" nailed creativity inside its coffin. A bad pun at best, the song was a Sid Vicious leftover from the part-time combo Flowers of Romance. Although Rotten overhauled Vicious's lyrics, the point he was left trying to make—that the genocide of a race was no joke—had been made with less ambiguity and a whole lot more economy [*sic*] in two lines of "Holidays in the Sun"—"I don't want a holiday in the sun / I wanna go to the new Belsen"—lines that were apparently still ambiguous enough to get the song banned by Capital Radio. With "Belsen Was a Gas," the Pistols would have needed the hoopla of controversy to make their mark because the song itself was not about to walk tall. The controversies that had stalked "Anarchy in the UK," "God

Save the Queen," "Holidays in the Sun," and *Bollocks* had been secondary to the Sound and Fury.

Although the Pistols never properly recorded "Belsen Was a Gas" in the studio, their roadie, with the evocative name of Boogie, apparently loused up a half-hearted attempt at a rough demo. Indeed the Pistols would never enter a studio again, although their "final" original would appear on their not-so-grand epitaph, *The Great Rock & Roll Swindle*—an EP disguised as a double-album—in two incarnations. One was an embarrassing Jones/Cook collaboration with exiled bankrobber Ronnie Biggs, and the other was from the Pistols' final gig at the Winterland Ballroom in San Francisco, recorded on the night of January 14, 1978. With their bassist out of the live mix, well actually just plain out of it, the sound is stripped of muscle. Rotten sounds tired of the whole circus, the all-too-real confines of a public image perhaps applying an even greater burden than the straightjacket of sound to which he would be bound as long as Jones and Cook remained his keepers.

Dancing on his own grave, Rotten ridiculed it all—the band, the hype, the paying punters—and delivered the most public epitaph since The Beatles called the final track on their last album "The End," as the finale to their last gig at Winterland: "Ha ha ha. Ever get the feeling you've been cheated? G'night." It was left to the *Telegraph,* the daily paper bought by those who believe that they should be running the country, to deliver the perfect obituary:

> The Sex Pistols, "punk rock's" answer to music, have broken up
> with all the dignity and good taste for which they are world famous.
> "Everyone just kicked each other in the teeth and we went our separate
> ways," said their manager Mr Malcolm McLaren, 31.

Unfortunately, at this point McLaren also showed such a fundamental misunderstanding of the ergonomics of Rock—"I think the spearhead group of punk rock has done what it set out to do, it has destroyed the myth of rock & roll superstardom"—that one has to question how much of the Pistols' trailblazing career was simply the compound of a series of McLaren stunts misfiring.

THE REPUTE OF BOLLOCKS

Never Mind the Bollocks has survived the revisionists, the post-revision-ists, and the post-post-revisionists of punk history (take a bow, Jon Savage and Legs McNeil). The final irony is that it is the inclusion of the four singles—an inclusion that brought the wrath of a nation of punk-purists down upon the band at the time—that has ensured the album's continuing importance, indeed landmark status, affecting all shades of the rock constituency.

In 1985, *Sounds* compiled their all-time top hundred albums and singles. The Pistols' great triumvirate of 45s occupied three of the top five slots—numbers 1, 3, and 5—"Anarchy" at 1, "GSTQ" at 3, and "Pretty Vacant" at 5. ("Holidays in the Sun"—championed by American critics like Paul Williams and Dave Marsh in their own selections of top singles—did not even make the nether regions of the *Sounds* hundred.) *Never Mind the Bollocks* was only nudged off the top spot by The Clash debut long-player.

A year later, *NME* repeated the exercise with its own roster of rock-crits, coming up with a somewhat more plausible list that recognized rock did not begin with punk (i.e., *Blood on the Tracks* appears, and Alan Vega's 1983 solo album *Saturn Strip* does not). Still, it placed *Never Mind the Bollocks* at a respectable number 13 in the pantheon, though *The Clash,* an album not even released in a recognizable form in the United States, again won the battle of punk platters, coming in at number 4.

Finally, *Rolling Stone* decided to celebrate its own twentieth anniver-sary in 1987 with an issue devoted to "The 100 Best Albums of the Last

Randy Enterprises ☆☆☆
PRESENTS
The most famous band in the world
AT
CROMER LINKS PAVILION
SATURDAY 24th DECEMBER
The SEX PISTOLS
Admission by Ticket Only ——— £1·75
DOORS OPEN 6·45 p.m. ● PERFORMANCE 8·00 p.m.
In order that you may witness the above happening and
move on to other festivities, the concert will finish at 9·00 p.m.
TICKETS AVAILABLE :- THE BOX OFFICE, CROMER CINEMA
Randie

Twenty Years." Predictably, it gave the top spot to an album slaughtered on the day of release by both the *New York Times* (Richard Goldstein) and the London *Times* (Nik Cohn), *Sergeant Pepper's Lonely Hearts Club Band.* Although *Bollocks* does not sound half the dated curio that *Pepper* now does, it again had to settle for that number two slot. However, the two-page *Rolling Stone* account, riddled as it is with inaccuracies ("it contained all three of the group's singles"; "*Bollocks* took about a month to record," etc.), at least recognized, and stated at the outset, the import of *Never Mind the Bollocks:*

> Nothing in rock was ever quite the same after *Never Mind the Bollocks.* The Sex Pistols swept away the crazy, corporate musical verites of the 1970s in a tidal wave of spit and derision. To the over-cranked velocity of the Ramones (an American band they admired [*sic*]), the Pistols added a profound contempt for all things phony and overinflated in the established culture—from jet-set rock stars to the reigning monarch of their native Britain.

As to why *Bollocks* became both the band's legacy and its epitaph, Steve Jones appositely summed it up at the end of the *Rolling Stone* piece:

I'm sure if we woulda stayed together, we could've been the biggest thing since sliced bread. But at the time the only thing I wanted to do was to fucking get out of it. It was drivin' me nuts. We wasn't writin' any songs. I didn't like John's attitudes toward music. Sid was gettin' more and more into junk and wasn't playin'. And all me and Paul really wanted to do was rock, you know?

In the 15 months after Winterland, Rotten and his new cohorts in PiL would come up with the magnificent *First Issue,* an album that certainly didn't share Jones's "attitude toward music"; Glen Matlock's Rich Kids would make one badly produced album of powerpop and call it a day; and Jones would spend hours and hours redubbing new parts onto the flotsam of the Pistols' studio career for that supposed soundtrack album, *The Great Rock & Roll Swindle.* Sid Vicious would be found, on the morning of February 1, 1979, "slumped up against the drain / with a whole lot of nothing running through his veins" ("Johnny Bye Bye," by Bruce Springsteen).

THE SONGS

Did You No Wrong
(NIGHTINGALE / JONES / MATLOCK / COOK / ROTTEN)
STUDIO RECORDINGS: WESSEX STUDIOS, MARCH 1977 ["GOD SAVE THE QUEEN" B-SIDE; *KISS THIS*]

FIRST DOCUMENTED LIVE PERFORMANCE: WELWYN GARDEN CITY, FEBRUARY 21, 1976.*

The one "original" to be retained from the days when the band's lineup was Paul Cook, Steve Jones, Wally Nightingale, and Glen Matlock, "Did You No Wrong" was the Pistols' regular set-opener through June 1976 and, though dropped at this point, reappeared later in the year—in August at Screen on the Green, in September at Chelmsford Security Prison, and November at the Notre Dame Hall, when London Weekend Television was filming the show for a half-hour punk documentary. It would also be selected as the B-side to "God Save the Queen." Jones and Cook couldn't resist laying down a version of the one Pistols original to feature Cook–Rotten lyrics at the March Wessex sessions. The second verse originally suggested a little wishful thinking on Cook's part:

> *I had a mind-bending trip around the USA,*
> *Running after you trying to find a way,*
> *To bring you back home with me,*
> *Got you in my arms, try and make you see.*

Rotten, though, "changed the lyrics because I didn't like the niceties of the song" (see Lee Woods's *Day by Day*).

He made it into some kind of a *News of the World* epic: "I ain't seen you up on the screen/ But those films are in my dream," suggests the lady in question is no longer able to fulfill our hero's (warped?) fantasies.

Seventeen
(JONES / MATLOCK / ROTTEN / COOK)

FIRST DOCUMENTED LIVE PERFORMANCE: WELWYN GARDEN CITY, FEBRUARY 21, 1976.*

STUDIO RECORDINGS: DENMARK STREET, JULY 1976 [*THE MINI ALBUM; EARLY DAZE; NO FUTURE UK; THIS IS CRAP*]; WESSEX STUDIOS, APRIL/MAY 1977 [*NEVER MIND THE BOLLOCKS*]; WESSEX STUDIOS, APRIL/MAY 1977 [*THIS IS CRAP*]

A staple of the Pistols repertoire from day one, "Seventeen" neatly summarized the outlook of a teenage wastrel with time on his hands, but not on his side. Originally entitled "Lazy Sod," the opening lines were, "You're only twenty-nine, Got a lot to learn/ but when your business dies, you will not return." It was changed on *Bollocks,* to the infinitely more vicious, "But when your mummy dies, she will not return." This line would come back to haunt Rotten when his mother died of cancer in 1979. "Seventeen" remains the Pistols' most pithy statement on "dole" (welfare) culture.

Pretty Vacant
(JONES / MATLOCK / ROTTEN / COOK)

FIRST DOCUMENTED LIVE PERFORMANCE: WELWYN GARDEN CITY, FEBRUARY 21, 1976.*

STUDIO RECORDINGS: MAJESTIC STUDIO, MAY 15, 1976 [*THIS IS CRAP*]; DENMARK STREET, JULY 1976 [*THE MINI ALBUM MK.2; NO FUTURE UK; WANTED: THE GOODMAN TAPES*]; GOOSEBERRY STUDIOS, JANUARY 17–20, 1977 [*EARLY DAZE; SPUNK* [W/ INTRO]; *NO FUTURE UK; THIS IS CRAP*]; WESSEX STUDIOS, MARCH 3–4, 1977 [A-SIDE; *NEVER MIND THE BOLLOCKS; KISS THIS*]

"Pretty Vacant" is the one song the Pistols (actually Matlock) wrote that had a definite connection with New York, even if it was only a song title by proxy. (The Pistols didn't hear Hell's "Blank Generation" until November 1976, when the Stiff EP was released.) Written in 1975, shortly after McLaren's return from New York and his mistimed, misdirected attempt to manage the by-then dissolute Dolls, Matlock took all the elements that first inspired the Pistols—the attitude of American punk, the drive of the 1960s BritInvasion singles, and a certain glam-pop sensibility that was about the only thing interesting then happening on the UK charts—and came up with something all his own.

GLEN MATLOCK: *"Pretty Vacant" [is] the only song I wrote entirely by myself. The idea for it came from a poster that Malcolm had brought back from the States, a small handbill for a Richard Hell Television gig with the titles of several songs scattered across it. One of the songs . . . was "(I Belong to the) Blank Generation." . . . As soon as I saw that I thought: that's the kind of feeling that we want to get across in our songs. . . . The Blank Generation idea was also linked to discussions we'd be having around the band. . . . From the beginning, the important thing was to get across the idea of the band in the songs of the band. We had to turn meaning into sound . . . the lyrics to "Pretty Vacant" . . . are mine, apart from a couple of lines that John later changed in the second verse ["Forget your cheap comments / we know we're for real."] . . . What I needed was one particular musical idea which would echo the lyrical idea. Finally that riff came to me in Moonies. . . . I was in there one lunchtime drinking my way through that week's dole money when Abba's "SOS" came on the jukebox. . . . The chord sequence for the chorus . . . came straight from The Small Faces' "Wham Bam, Thank You Ma'am."*

Submission

(JONES / MATLOCK / ROTTEN / COOK)

FIRST DOCUMENTED LIVE PERFORMANCE: WELWYN GARDEN CITY, FEBRUARY 21, 1976.*

STUDIO RECORDINGS: DENMARK STREET, JULY 1976 [*THE MINI ALBUM; EARLY DAZE; NO FUTURE UK; THIS IS CRAP; WANTED: THE GOODMAN TAPES*]; WESSEX STUDIOS, APRIL/MAY 1977 [*NEVER MIND THE BOLLOCKS*]; WESSEX STUDIOS, JUNE (?) 1977 [*THIS IS CRAP*]

"Submission," the "torch ballad" (cough) in the Pistols live set that allowed audiences to catch their collective breath before the mayhem of "Vacant," "Problems," "No Fun," and "Anarchy," may have taken its guitar riff wholesale from The Kinks, but the song's main instigators, Rotten and Matlock, were actually trying to create something more referential to The Doors.

JOHNNY ROTTON: *We were in Camden Town rehearsing at the Roundhouse for a small period. The arguments between Glen and me became severe by this time. Malcolm finally insisted we go to a small pub upstairs and sit down and work it all out. We did. We*

*were given twenty quid to sit down and get drunk and put our dif-
ferences aside. . . . The Doors was the common ground—we found
a band that we, shockingly, both liked.*

The song's title was another joke at McLaren's expense. Matlock and
Rotten were being pushed to write an S&M anthem but came up instead
with a song about a submarine mission (Sub Mission, geddit). Of course,
the underwater imagery, tied as it is to the notion of drowning in her love,
suggests the all-consuming, gurgling acquiescence a submissive in love
may feel, though the uptight, lapsed Catholic inside Rotten was bound to
want to put such a notion in code, radar blips et al.

New York
(Jones / Matlock / Rotten / Cook)

First documented live performance:
Welwyn Garden City, February 21,
1976.*

Studio Recordings: Gooseberry Studios, January 17–20, 1977 [*Early Daze; No
Future UK; This Is Crap*]; Wessex Studios, April/May 1977 [*Never Mind the
Bollocks*]

———

Johnny Rotten: *The only thing anybody knew about this so-called
New York scene was what Malcolm would tell us.*

Paul Cook: *We thought we could do it better and we did.*

Much has been made of the Pistols' so-called affiliations with the New
York scene. In fact, Rotten had nothing but contempt for most "Noo
Yawk" music, Patti Smith and The Ramones (the only two CBGBs acts
whose debuts precede the Pistols) included. At the June 1976
Manchester show, during "New York," Rotten launches into a tirade
against "that slut" Patti Smith, whose two Roundhouse shows two weeks
earlier had been so roundly praised by the UK music press. McLaren's
obsession with The New York Dolls not only resulted in endless piss-
takin', London-style, but also inspired the Pistols to pen this claim to
autonomy from other garage sounds. This claim "inspired" Johnny
Thunders of Dolls fame to pen his own oh-so-lame retort, "London Boys."

Satellite
(Jones / Matlock / Rotten / Cook)

First documented live performance:
Nashville Rooms, West Kensington,
April 3, 1976.

STUDIO RECORDINGS: DENMARK STREET, JULY 1976 [*THE MINI ALBUM; EARLY DAZE; NO FUTURE UK; THIS IS CRAP; WANTED: THE GOODMAN TAPES*]; WESSEX STUDIOS, APRIL/MAY AND AUGUST 1977 [*THIS IS CRAP*]; WESSEX STUDIOS, APRIL/MAY 1977 ["HOLIDAYS IN THE SUN" B-SIDE; *KISS THIS*]

According to Rotten, "Satellite" was "the story of the travelling nonsense [involved in gigging] and picking up enough money to survive for a day or two. We had to do it. . . . As bad as it was in London for young people, they had nothing at all in the satellite towns. No social scene, nothing." Certainly, the references in the song to a "satellite kid / you got no name . . . you got no brain / I bet you're all so happy in suburbia dream," may tie in with Rotten's latter-day view, though the song quickly advances to an attack on someone "try[ing] to join the scene / but you're too obscene." According to Matlock, "Satellite" was intended to be an abusive depiction of an obscure object of desire for the young Lydon ("there ain't no bid for your chastity"). The lady in question, Shanne Bradley, described in the song as a "big, fat pink baked-bean," subsequently formed the Nipple Erectors. Bradley herself recently recalled this rotten relationship (to Nina Antonia) in somewhat innocuous terms:

> I was an art student and I went to St. Albans [College]. . . . The Pistols gate-crashed a party there. We thought they were crap but I got talking to them afterwards. They couldn't really play very well and we were taking the piss out of them. This was the autumn of 1975. I was dressed up in an outsize granny's corset, I had a holster with a gun. I'd chopped all my hair off, henna'd it and then peroxide'd it so it was bright orange like a nylon rug. So I looked like they did. It was my own rebellion against looking nice. . . . The Pistols came up to me because I looked that way. I asked them their names and when John said Rotten I thought he was taking the piss. He had this big mohair jumper on. I said, "I like your jumper." He showed me the label. It said Sex. . . . There was an exchange of phone numbers between John and me. He said I should go to the shop and have a look at the clothes. He said he worked there some of the time but when I went there he wasn't there. . . . I met John again at the ICA. McLaren and Westwood were giving a talk about their clothes. But we just sat at the bar drinking coffee.

Problems
(JONES / MATLOCK / ROTTEN / COOK)

FIRST DOCUMENTED LIVE PERFORMANCE:
NASHVILLE ROOMS, WEST KENSINGTON,
APRIL 3, 1976.

STUDIO RECORDINGS: MAJESTIC STUDIO, MAY 15, 1976 [*THIS IS CRAP; PIRATES OF DESTINY*]; MANCHESTER SQUARE, LONDON, DECEMBER 1976; GOOSEBERRY STUDIOS, JANUARY 17–20, 1977 [*EARLY DAZE; NO FUTURE UK; THIS IS CRAP*]; WESSEX STUDIOS, APRIL/MAY 1977 [*NEVER MIND THE BOLLOCKS*]

———

One of the most recorded of Pistols originals, "Problems" was actually conceived one day at rehearsals out of a feeling of general entropy (Johnny Rotten: "We had run out of songs") and a single word, intoned in Rotten's best Dalek-voice: "Problem." This duosyllabic rant became the Pistols' favorite set-closer, though it is one of the Pistols' less structured works, betraying its origins in an afternoon jam beset by problems . . . problems . . . problems.

No Feelings
(JONES / MATLOCK / ROTTEN / COOK)

FIRST DOCUMENTED LIVE PERFORMANCE:
NASHVILLE ROOMS, WEST KENSINGTON,
APRIL 3, 1976.

STUDIO RECORDINGS: MAJESTIC STUDIO, MAY 15, 1976 [*THIS IS CRAP; PIRATES OF DESTINY*]; DENMARK STREET, JULY 1976 [*THE MINI ALBUM; EARLY DAZE; NO FUTURE UK; THIS IS CRAP*]; MANCHESTER SQUARE, LONDON, DECEMBER 1976; WESSEX STUDIOS, APRIL/MAY 1977 [*NEVER MIND THE BOLLOCKS*]; WESSEX STUDIOS, APRIL/MAY 1977 [*THIS IS CRAP*]

———

Though not the first pop song to reflect back on its subject, "No Feelings" may still be Rotten's finest lyric, a remarkable mini-treatise on the desensitized self and life in towerblockland. Kicking off in a suspiciously awry love song mode, "I saw you in the mirror when the story began / I fell in love with you, I love your mortal sin," the song soon turns in on itself with "I got no emotion for anybody else / better understand I'm in love with myself." Possibly its original spark [*sic*] was a 1974 cut, "Guess I'm Falling in Love with Myself Again" by Sparks, but "No Feelings" remains punk's definitive expression of teen misanthropy. "No Feelings" would be recorded by Chris Spedding, Dave Goodman, Mike Thorne, and Bill Price before it was deemed releasable, though structurally it barely ever changed from its May 1976 guise.

Flowers of Romance
(JONES / MATLOCK / ROTTEN / COOK)

FIRST DOCUMENTED LIVE PERFORMANCE: 100
CLUB, OXFORD STREET, LONDON, JUNE 29,
1976.

STUDIO RECORDINGS: NO STUDIO RECORDING KNOWN.

Not so much a song as a deliberately unfocused retort, "Flowers of Romance" was the Pistols' way of debunking the word on the wire that these boys couldn't play. Opening with such a cacophonous racket, over which Rotten could cast his aspersions far and wide, the remainder of the set was bound to sound positively harmonic (a trick learned from the Velvets). "Flowers" seems to have only survived a couple of months, being last performed, in much abbreviated form, as an intro to "Pretty Vacant" at their August Bank Holiday 100 Club return.

Wanna Be Me
(Jones / Matlock / Rotten / Cook)

First documented live performance: 100 Club, Oxford Street, London, June 29, 1976.

Studio Recordings: Denmark Street, July 1976 ["Anarchy in the UK" B-side; *The Great Rock & Roll Swindle* MK.2; *Kiss This; The Mini Album; Early Daze; No Future UK; This Is Crap*]

Some, notably Jon Savage, have tried to apply "I Wanna Be Me" to a very specific target, "a 'typewriter god' suspiciously like [*NME* scribe] Nick Kent." However, although Kent had once auditioned for the Pistols, he never exacted his sense of disappointment at failing the audition in print. The occasion when Kent was attacked with a bike chain by Sid Vicious, some weeks after "I Wanna Be Me" was written, appears to have been a purely spontaneous act of thuggery on the part of Vicious. For "I Wanna Be Me," Rotten has surely taken a far greater body of wannabes to task. By June 1976, it must have been quite galling for the band to have to read the same tired hacks talking about "musicality." "I Wanna Be Me" turns the debate on its head, asking hard questions about what exactly it is that these rock critics want of the Pistols and their kind. Young, brash, and ready to take on the world, Rotten believes that "you wanna be me," and, perhaps in this at least, he may have had the starstruck Kent in mind. "I Wanna Be Me" was only recorded once, less than three weeks after the song had been written. Yet it remained a perennial in the live set, often exacting Rotten's most vituperative vocal of the evening. It would be fair to say he has never entirely forgiven the music press.

Anarchy in the UK
(Jones / Matlock / Rotten / Cook)

First documented live performance: Lesser Free Trade Hall, Manchester, July 20, 1976 [no known recording available].

STUDIO RECORDINGS: DENMARK STREET, JULY 1976 [*THE MINI ALBUM; EARLY DAZE; NO FUTURE UK; THIS IS CRAP*]; WESSEX STUDIOS, OCTOBER 1976 [*THE GREAT ROCK & ROLL SWINDLE; NO FUTURE UK; THIS IS CRAP*]; WESSEX STUDIOS, LATE OCTOBER/EARLY NOVEMBER 1976 [A-SIDE; *NEVER MIND THE BOLLOCKS; KISS THIS*]

More tape would be expended on "Anarchy in the UK" than any other Pistols song, mostly in the solitary month of October 1976. First recorded in July 1976, "Anarchy in the UK" was truly a collaborative effort. Jones had been giving Matlock some ill-directed gyp about a "theme song" he had been threatening to write, when Matlock came up with "the whole chord sequence—there and then." Rotten produced "these amazing lyrics half an hour later," while Jones did what he could do best, "turned up the guitar and thrashed away." The July 1976 demo shows a song still edging its way toward catharsis, but over the suceeding months the song would become a beacon of fury, introducing show after show (and often capping them as well, in second encore guise), Jones's ringing feedback still tickling the lobes long after the band had started on the rider. The original version recorded for EMI best illustrates the song's live path, but the slicker, more honed version, produced by Thomas and issued by EMI, would still give mid-1970s rock the punk equivalent of the Heimlich maneuver. As Paul Williams put it: "It is as bold as Elvis in his brief shining moment. It doesn't just give the finger to the powers that be. It screams in their faces, demanding response (and dismissing that response before hearing it)."

Liar
(JONES / MATLOCK / ROTTEN / COOK)

FIRST DOCUMENTED LIVE PERFORMANCE: BARBARELLAS, BIRMINGHAM, AUGUST 14, 1976.**

STUDIO RECORDINGS: MANCHESTER SQUARE, LONDON, DECEMBER 1976; GOOSEBERRY STUDIOS, JANUARY 17–20, 1977 [*EARLY DAZE; NO FUTURE UK; THIS IS CRAP*]; WESSEX STUDIOS, APRIL/MAY 1977 [*NEVER MIND THE BOLLOCKS*]

After the spurt of inspiration that resulted in "Anarchy" and "I Wanna Be Me," both in June, stagnation in the songwriting department set in, coinciding with the Pistols finding their groove on stage. By then, their fury was no longer directed at the equipment, at each other, or the audience, but rather at the songs and their subject matter. In the five months between the penning of "Anarchy" and "No Future," the Pistols would introduce just one song into their set, the quite lame "Liar." According to

Cook, this was one of the earliest songs Matlock and Rotten worked on together. If so, it had been shuffled to the bottom of the pack, emerging only when good cards were not flowing so freely. The riff is straight out of the Steve Jones book of chugs, but once the band has joined him in the maelstrom, he is reaching for the rope. The lyrics, for once, are not concerned with the salvation of the young, not even the salvation of annihilation, but betray the camp bitchiness of cliquedom, a snare that would soon wholly restrain the impressionable Mr. Lydon. At this point, Lydon clearly thought he could always be the gamemaster, "I think you're funny, you're funny, ha, ha/ I don't need you, don't need your blah blah."

God Save the Queen
(JONES / MATLOCK / ROTTEN / COOK)

FIRST DOCUMENTED LIVE PERFORMANCE: HENDON POLYTECHNIC, NOVEMBER 19, 1976 [NO KNOWN RECORDING AVAILABLE].
STUDIO RECORDINGS: MANCHESTER SQUARE, LONDON, DECEMBER 1976 [*AGRESSION THRU REPRESSION* BOOTLEG CD]; GOOSEBERRY STUDIOS, JANUARY 17–20, 1977 [*EARLY DAZE; NO FUTURE UK; THIS IS CRAP*]; WESSEX STUDIOS, MARCH 3–4, 1977 [A-SIDE; *NEVER MIND THE BOLLOCKS; KISS THIS*]

"God Save the Queen" caused problems, internal and external, from day one. Sprouting from a melody Matlock had created at the piano to pass the time at the Goodman "Anarchy" sessions, Rotten once again pulled out a set of lyrics he'd kept to himself awaiting an appropriate partner-in-crime.

> JOHNNY ROTTEN: *The words didn't fit in with any of the other tunes. I didn't think it would ever fit to anything. It was more like a big tirade.*

"No Future" was the way the song was introduced at shows on the "Anarchy" tour. Premiered at a show at Hendon Poly, the Pistols were given little opportunity to hone the song before they cut their first demo of it with Mike Thorne. A month later, Goodman got his turn, but the March 1977 Thomas recording would never be bettered, either in the studio or on stage, even though it was, according to Jones, "recorded after just two takes, with guitar and drums [only]."

EMI
(JONES / MATLOCK / ROTTEN / COOK)

FIRST DOCUMENTED LIVE PERFORMANCE: NOTRE DAME HALL, LEICESTER SQUARE, LONDON, MARCH 21, 1977 [NO KNOWN RECORDING AVAILABLE].

STUDIO RECORDINGS: GOOSEBERRY STUDIOS, JANUARY 17–20, 1977 [*EARLY DAZE; NO FUTURE UK; THIS IS CRAP*]; WESSEX STUDIOS, MARCH/APRIL 1977 [*NEVER MIND THE BOLLOCKS*]; WESSEX STUDIOS, MARCH/APRIL 1977 [*THIS IS CRAP*]

Hoofed off EMI on January 6, the Pistols wrapped up their first studio rendition of this scathing tirade before EMI even officially terminated their contract on January 22. According to Matlock, "the tune is largely Jones." The words are pure, undiluted Rotten: "Unlimited supply/ and there is no reason why/ they told us it was all a frame/ They only did it 'cause of fame. Who?" Before the song was even debuted live, Matlock had quit, taking his "EMI" bassline with him, and the "unlimited supply" offered by A&M proved just as illusory as EMI's. "Hello EMI, goodbye . . . A&M."

Holidays in the Sun
(JONES / COOK / ROTTEN / VICIOUS)

FIRST DOCUMENTED LIVE PERFORMANCE: "THE QUEEN ELIZABETH," RIVER THAMES, LONDON, JUNE 7, 1977.
STUDIO RECORDINGS: WESSEX STUDIOS, JUNE 1977 [A-SIDE; *NEVER MIND THE BOLLOCKS; KISS THIS*]

> JOHNNY ROTTEN: *I loved that [Berlin] wall and the insanity of the place. Twenty-four hours of chaotic fun. It was geared up to annoy the Russians. West Berlin at the time was inside the communist state of East Germany. It was a fairground with only one airport and one motorway leading into it—surrounded by downtrodden, dull, gray, military-minded bastards who live thoroughly miserable lives. They looked in on this circus atmosphere of West Berlin—which never went to sleep—and that would be their impression of the West.*

"Holidays in the Sun" suggests that Rotten's lyrical skills were advancing just as the Pistols' oft-ridiculed musicality was beating a hasty retreat. With a riff copped straight from the recently charted debut Jam single "In the City," and the fearsome scrunch of jackboots triggering a bass-drum march, the cavalcade of images Rotten brings to the song almost obscures the sheer repetitiveness of the guitar tracks (and their bass twin). Written in March, when a trip to the Channel Isles was derailed and the boys somehow ended up in Berlin, the song begins with Rotten projecting his own reluctance to view "the new Belsen," before the narrator is unwittingly transported behind the Iron Curtain, required to peer over the Berlin Wall and build up a picture postcard of life in the West based on what he sees. At song's end, as he desperately seeks to climb back over the wall, and Jones's guitar attack at last begins to fire something other than blanks, Rotten turns agnostic, falling to his knees and praying, "Please don't be waiting for me!"

Bodies
(JONES / COOK / ROTTEN / VICIOUS)

FIRST DOCUMENTED LIVE PERFORMANCE: EKSIT CLUB, ROTTERDAM, HOLLAND, DECEMBER 5, 1977 [NO KNOWN RECORDING AVAILABLE ***].

STUDIO RECORDINGS: WESSEX STUDIOS, AUGUST 1977 [*NEVER MIND THE BOLLOCKS*]

> JOHNNY ROTTEN: *Pauline was a girl who used to send these letters to me from some nuthouse up north in Birmingham. She was in a mental asylum. She turned up at my door once wearing a see-through plastic bag. . . . The fetus thing is what got me.*

In "Bodies" Rotten once again revels in his own moral ambivalence. The last track recorded for *Bollocks,* and a song they presumably deliberately refrained from debuting on the SPOTS tour, even though it had already been recorded, "Bodies" is not a simplistic anti-abortion rant, the taboo of taboos within the Catholic creed Rotten had been born to but had done so much to disavow. It is as much about self-hate, and revulsion at one-self, "She don't want a baby that looks like that . . . fuck it all, and fuck the fucking brat." And yet, intercut at Chris Thomas's suggestion is a third-person point of view, and suddenly it is Lydon the frontman who points an accusing finger: "She was a no-one who killed her baby." As his most powerful witness, he calls the very fetus that Pauline in real life apparently carried around in a plastic bag attached to her neck. He damns Pauline with the most "human" of cries at song's end, "I'm not an animal . . . Mummy!"

Belsen Was a Gas
(JONES / COOK / ROTTEN / VICIOUS)

FIRST DOCUMENTED LIVE PERFORMANCE: EKSIT CLUB, ROTTERDAM, HOLLAND, DECEMBER 5, 1977 [NO KNOWN RECORDING AVAILABLE ***].

STUDIO RECORDINGS: NO STUDIO RECORDING KNOWN.

The one Pistols song to bear the neanderthal imprint of Vicious, "Belsen Was a Gas" apparently was originally coauthored by Vicious and Keith Levene (soon to be Rotten's next important collaborator in PiL), members of an amorphous ensemble called Flowers of Romance, who used up London rehearsal space in the autumn of 1976. Rotten wisely decided that the words needed a tad more irony, the Vicious original lacking any such sense in its depiction of the concentration camp. Rotten retained Vicious's original opening: "Belsen was a gas / I read the other day / in the open graves / where the Jews all lay." However, Rotten then switched his attention to the guards whose silent complicity in the barbarity could not be excused, "Be a man, kill someone," Rotten suggests and then, more helpfully, "KILL YOURSELF!" Never recorded in the studio, "Belsen Was a Gas" drew much comment on its introduction into the set in December 1977. The stunned silence at the end of the Winterland performance suggests that this was one taboo that the Pistols had been unwise to breach.

The Covers

Understanding
(MARRIOTT / LANE)

FIRST DOCUMENTED LIVE PERFORMANCE: WELWYN GARDEN CITY, FEBRUARY 21, 1976.*

STUDIO RECORDINGS: NO STUDIO RECORDING KNOWN.

One of two Small Faces "covers" in the early Pistols' live repertoire, "Understanding" had originally seen the light of day back in 1966, as the B-side of "All or Nothing," the Faces' only number one single. The impact of The Small Faces, the Decca-era Faces (1965–1966) in particular, on the Pistols can best be gauged by the songs they rehearsed in the couple of months before their live debut, which included no less than five Faces covers: the four 1966 singles, "Sha La La La Lee," "Hey Girl," "All or Nothing," "My Mind's Eye," plus "Understanding." Although "Understanding" was the only one from this quintet to make it into the live set, it was soon joined by a rewritten "Watcha Gonna Do About It." "Understanding" remained in the Pistols' repertoire until April 1976, when it was asked to make way for some new originals. As a cry for understanding— "You got to do this thing with feeling / You got to know just what I'm meaning/ You got to believe just what I'm handing . . . understanding"—Rotten presumably deemed the song not confrontational enough to share the stage with "No Feelings," "Problems," "Steppin' Stone," and so on.

Watcha Gonna Do About It
(SAMWELL / POTTER)

FIRST DOCUMENTED LIVE PERFORMANCE: WELWYN GARDEN CITY, FEBRUARY 21, 1976.*

If "Understanding" got the push early on because it did not turn angst to anger, "Watcha Gonna Do About It," which obdurately retained its place, was party to a Pistol-style paint job. A-side to The Small Faces' debut single, "Watcha Gonna Do About It" professed unrequited desire, requesting the object of affection to do something about it. Rotten, however, was not about to evince a bothersome emotion like lurve (or even lust, having memorably dismissed sex as "two minutes and a half minutes of squelching noises,") and gave the song his own, unique spin: "I wantcha to know that I HATE you baby / Wantcha to know I DON'T care." Verse two continued in the same vein: "I want you to know that you're rotten, baby / I am Rotten too [Matlock: Oh, yes he is, babe]." A highlight at many an early show, the song was axed after the June Manchester show, in favor of the newly written "I Wanna Be Me." However, during the interminable Wessex sessions, "Watcha Gonna Do About It" was wheeled out for reinspection. Unfortunately, although everyone seems happy enough to give the song a go, 90 seconds in Rotten can't even remember the second verse, the musicians seem thoroughly pissed off, and Rotten starts (b)itching to do "No Fun." Despite having "outtake" writ large over it, the Wessex version was originally included on *The Great Rock & Roll Swindle,* was then deleted in favor of "I Wanna Be Me" (appropriately enough), and has now been reinstated on the current release.

Substitute
(TOWNSHEND)

FIRST DOCUMENTED LIVE PERFORMANCE: WELWYN GARDEN CITY, FEBRUARY 21, 1976.*

STUDIO RECORDINGS: WESSEX STUDIOS, OCTOBER 1976 [*GREAT ROCK & ROLL SWINDLE; PIRATES OF DESTINY*]

"Substitute" was the Pistols' most audacious selection in their personal jukebox of covers. A true classic, untarnished by years on replay, "Substitute," originally issued by The Who in 1966, was the followup to "My Generation" and the first indication that Townshend was emerging as a writer of a peculiarly English type. "I look pretty white but my dad was black / My mohair suit is really made out of sack," was certainly an audacious couplet for a 1966 pop song. As the one song a casual punter who unwittingly encountered the 1976 Pistols would almost certainly know, "Substitute" lasted through the "Anarchy" tour and was forsaken only when it became one more song Vicious couldn't play. *The Great Rock & Roll Swindle* take—again from the Wessex "covers" session—zings along well enough for Rotten to comment at song's end, "Now that was good" (audible on *Pirates of Destiny* but one of the many sounds mixed out on *The Swindle*).

(I'm Not Your) Steppin' Stone
(BOYCE / HART)

FIRST DOCUMENTED LIVE PERFORMANCE: WELWYN GARDEN CITY, FEBRUARY 21, 1976.*

STUDIO RECORDINGS: WESSEX STUDIOS, OCTOBER 1976 [*GREAT ROCK & ROLL SWINDLE*; *PIRATES OF DESTINY*]

"(I'm Not Your) Steppin' Stone" was a most curious choice for a B-side by the Monkees, a fabricated foursome conjured up by NBC executives to sitcomize The Beatles. That it was placed on the rear of the Monkees' biggest hit, "I'm a Believer," makes for one of the most incongruous pairings in pop history. Blending elements of the Stones' "Play with Fire" and Dylan's "Like a Rolling Stone," "Steppin' Stone" is a white trash monologue directed at a social-climber par excellence. As such, the fact that the two leading lights of underground rock in the fall of 1975, the Heartbreakers in New York and the Pistols in London, unconsciously but simultaneously adopted it perhaps suggests a song whose time had come. Certainly the words of the song were wasted, back in 1967, on the effete vocal chords of Mancunian Davey Jones. Only when Rotten copped his bilious laughing gear round the song did its black heart beat in time. Rotten once again couldn't resist a little lyrical tinkering, turning, "The clothes you're wearing, girl, are causing public scenes," into a reference to punk chic, "The clothes you're wearing, babe, they're falling at the seams." In 1979, another Wessex cover, "Steppin' Stone" would become the last single to bear the moniker, Sex Pistols.

(Don't You Give Me) No Lip
(J. D. THOMAS / RICHARDS)

FIRST DOCUMENTED LIVE PERFORMANCE: WELWYN GARDEN CITY, FEBRUARY 21, 1976.*

STUDIO RECORDINGS: WESSEX STUDIOS, OCTOBER 1976 [*GREAT ROCK & ROLL SWINDLE*; *PIRATES OF DESTINY*]

If the Pistols added a certain switchblade quality to the likes of "Steppin' Stone" and "Watcha Gonna Do About It," the Dave Berry who told some insolent prepubescent "Don't You Give Me No Lip Child" back in 1964 cannot have had the faintest inkling what behemoth would be unleashed when the song reached adulthood, twelve years on. Berry's slap on the wrist becomes one serious beating on the brat in the hands of Rotten. The B-side to Berry's best known single, "The Crying Game," "No Lip" was subject to such an overhaul by the Pistols, in particular by Matlock, whose distinctive bassline takes the song a whole lot further down the road to catharsis, that "Thomas–Richards arr. Matlock / Jones / Cook / Rotten" might have been a more just credit for its reincarnation. As it is, "No Lip" on *The Great Rock & Roll Swindle* retains very little of its original self, Jones burying Matlock and Rotten in a swathe of guitar overdubs. On the other hand, "No Lip" on *(Truly) Indecent Exposure* effortlessly conveys the knuckledusting the boys regularly gave Mr. Berry's original live.

No Fun
(THE STOOGES)

FIRST DOCUMENTED LIVE PERFORMANCE: WELWYN GARDEN CITY, FEBRUARY 21, 1976.*

STUDIO RECORDINGS: WESSEX STUDIOS, OCTOBER 1976 ["PRETTY VACANT" B-SIDE; *KISS THIS; NO FUTURE UK* (UNEDITED)]

The Pistols' most famous cover, "No Fun" was also their only nonoriginal that gave a nod across the pond. Although many an American rock critic has sought to daub the Pistols in the spirit of garageland USA, The Stooges (and, less significantly, the Dolls) remain the only obvious American pro cursors of style and sound. "No Fun," a two-chord kerrang from the first Elektra album, *The Stooges,* aka *1969,* clocked in at five minutes-plus on The Stooges' album, but rarely under six when disinterred for the climax of a Pistols set. The Pistols abandoned the sniff'n'groove approach of the original in favor of a resolute rock-out. The Stooges, on "No Fun," get by with some decidedly distant drums beating beneath the sound of two hands clapping. Whenever the Pistols did the song—i.e., at just about every gig where the Pistols got to finish their set—Cook led from the front, Rotten regularly delighting in taunting the audience in midsong, "You stand and stare/ grow your hair/ cut your flares/ you look so square . . . NAW FUNNN!!" The Wessex version, released as one-half of the perfect single, "Pretty Vacant," in July 1977, was another unscheduled cut at the

"Anarchy" sessions, liver than they would ever be again, and only belatedly supplanted as B-side to "Anarchy" by the demo of "I Wanna Be Me."

Johnny B. Goode
(C. BERRY)
FIRST DOCUMENTED LIVE PERFORMANCE:
NEVER PERFORMED LIVE.
STUDIO RECORDINGS: WESSEX STUDIOS, OCTOBER 1976 [*GREAT ROCK & ROLL SWINDLE; PIRATES OF DESTINY*]

———

"Johnny B. Goode," given its status at the very foundation of the rock pantheon and upbeat promise of stardom and potency for any such guitar player, seems a most unlikely choice for a Pistols cover. Indeed, Rotten sounds somewhat perturbed when (Jones?) makes the suggestion at Wessex, reluctantly giving the OK—"God! oh, alright then"—but changing his mind nanoseconds later as Jones signs his soul away with a single heavy metal riff and Rotten has to plead, "If you can swing . . . oh, fuck off . . . I don't know the words . . . oh fuck, it's awful, I hate songs like that, THE PITS!!" Jones and Cook pile along, oblivious to Rotten's disquiet, even when Chuck's signature tune is buried by 100 watts of power.

Roadrunner
(RICHMAN)
FIRST DOCUMENTED LIVE PERFORMANCE:
NEVER PERFORMED LIVE.
STUDIO RECORDINGS: WESSEX STUDIOS, OCTOBER 1976 [*GREAT ROCK & ROLL SWINDLE; PIRATES OF DESTINY*]

———

Another song that was worked up at rehearsals in the autumn of 1975 but was never performed by the Pistols (at least not until the "comeback" tour of 1996), "Roadrunner" had been the signature tune for Boston eccentric singer-songwriter Jonathan Richman since the 1971 debut of his Modern Lovers. The song was recorded at least three times in the studio in 1972, though the album Richman and company recorded that year with ex-Velvet founder John Cale would not be released until 1976. The version that Rotten and the boys took their cue from was a more muted rendition recorded in 1974, after the dissolution of the original Modern Lovers, and released on the various artists' sampler *Beserkley Chartbusters* the following year. A UK double A-side of the 1972 and 1974 versions of "Roadrunner" was issued in 1976, garnering enthusiastic airplay, particularly in London, ensuring that Richman was accorded punk-godfather status in the lead up to the revolution. The Wessex version stems from Rotten's desperate attempt to lead the band away from "Johnny B. Goode," but, as with the bulk of songs attempted at this "covers" session, it is Rotten's failure to remember more than a verse of lyrics that consigns "Roadrunner" to the trashcan (at least, until McLaren exhumed this particular garbage truck for his *Great Rock & Roll Swindle*).

Through My Eyes FIRST DOCUMENTED LIVE PERFORMANCE:
(GARNER / PHILLIPS) NEVER PERFORMED LIVE.
STUDIO RECORDINGS: WESSEX STUDIOS, OCTOBER 1976 [*PIRATES OF DESTINY*]

A fragment of The Creation single, "Through My Eyes" appears on *Pirates of Destiny,* the most dissolute of a fairly dilapidated bunch of covers from Wessex studios. Not even usable on as conspicuous an act of graverobbing as *The Great Rock & Roll Swindle,* the 1.37 it lasts is almost entirely taken up with Rotten berating the band for its inability to play the song, even though he can sing little more than the opening couplet himself, "No, do 'Through My Eyes.' I know how it goes. 'If you could see through my eyes/ you might be surprised . . .' C'mon do it. Oi, the worst it is the better, 'cause it's a load of shit anyway. . . . I know I used to, but I haven't heard it in years, and you couldn't play it . . . you remember, you could never get it right 'cause it was just such a weird tune, you'd have to be jumped up to do it." "Through My Eyes" had indeed been a regular at early Pistols rehearsals, although it remained as unperformed as other would-be nuggets like "Psychotic Reaction," "A Day Without Love," "I'm Not Like Everybody Else," and "I'm a Boy."

* According to Lee Woods's *Sex Pistols Day by Day,* there is a recording of the Pistols' gig at St. Albans two days earlier. However, the only St. Albans tape I have ever encountered was a "fake" edit, deriving from the Nashville April 3, 1976, show. Dated January 28, 1976, this "St. Albans tape" was issued on bootleg vinyl. I have never encountered a February 19, 1976, St. Albans tape that accords with the track-listing in *Day by Day,* and I have therefore assumed that the Welwyn Garden City tape remains the earliest known Pistols live recording until I hear audio evidence to the contrary.

** The inclusion of "Flowers of Romance" and the position of "Liar" in the set clearly suggests an August date and, as far as is known, the Pistols only played Barbarellas once, August 14, 1976. However, it sounds on the tape like someone is requesting "God Save the Queen" and Rotten is refusing to play it because they got in trouble the last time they played it, possibly a reference to a show at Lanchester Polytechnic in November. Nothing else on the tape, though, suggests such a late recording date.

*** There is a fine-quality tape of the Pistols' Dutch tour in circulation that may well derive from one of the first two or three shows (i.e., December 5–7). Since this twelve-song soundboard tape includes "Belsen Was a Gas," this undated recording would be the earliest known performance of their last composition. The full track-listing of the "Dutch Tour" tape runs thus: "God Save the Queen"; "I Wanna Be Me"; "Seventeen"; "New York"; "EMI"; "Bodies"; "Belsen Was a Gas"; "Holidays in the Sun"; "Problems"; "Pretty Vacant"; "Anarchy in the UK"; and "No Fun."

THE REVIEWS

Zigzag
DECEMBER 1977
BY KRIS NEEDS

The title says it all really. Ignore the press hysteria, dopey articles in *Rolling Stone* and cross-country panic/fear/loathing over "those foul-mouthed Sex Pistols." This album transcends it all . . . and also puts paid to the ignorant bastards who still say the Pistols can't play or are morons.

Even those who know the songs from gigs will be surprised at the sheer attack and overwhelming density of the sound—unlike a lot of groups the Pistols and producers Bill Price and Chris Thomas have got a killer sound right first time . . . but then I s'pose the songs have had time to mature and they weren't too proud to spend a bit of time in the studio to get it right. The result is a raging Berlin Wall of gut-wrenching power chords from Steve Jones, Paul Cook's simple and just right powerhouse drumming and the metronomic roar of Sid's bass. It's all topped with John's phenomenal voice, which can slide from spine-chilling no-feelings coldness to frenzied manic wailing.

He packs the maximum punch and effect into every syllable he delivers. I've never heard John in better form than his sneering whine on "EMI," a big raspberry to the two dopey record labels who stupidly let the Pistols plop from their grasp. Think of the lost Sales Units chaps. I hope it cuts you to the bone.

Yes, this is a direct, honest, no bullshit album which contains some of the most vital rock songs of this decade, brutal, real and full of energy and passion.

There's no danger of this album being ignored so this review ain't a mission of shared discovery, but in Zigzag's case there are probably a whole lot of readers from the previous era who will not even allow themselves to listen to this album because of the name of the group. Alright I'm not saying go out 'n' buy every single by every punk rock bandwagon-jumping shit combo, but please at least listen to NMTBHTSP cos it's great music in any books, and leaves most of the so-called New Wave standing at the starting-line.

Quick, here's the tracks . . .

HOLIDAYS IN THE SUN: Alright, so the riff's like "In the City" but I still reckon this is a corker and easily as good as anything the Pistols have done. I love the impenetrable sound wall and John's vocals, which have to fight to be heard in the guitar-and-drum maelstrom.

BODIES: Without a doubt my favorite track, apart from "EMI." Yes, the present Pistols line-up can still cut it in the song-writing stakes. This track is like a punch in the chops. It's definitely the most overpoweringly nasty, maybe even gross thing the group has done. But for this subject matter—a dead end factory girl from Birmingham's sordid abortion, it's gotta be.

Get these—

Dragged on a table in a factory
An illegitimate place to be
In a package in the lavatory
Died the little baby screaming
Body a screaming fucking bloody mess
Screamin

Screaming I'm not an animal in the chorus and ending on a chilling cry of "Mum!," Rotten makes a searing statement against abortion. More real and scary than the Pistols have ever been—a promising and reassuring pointer to the future. It also rocks like shit.

NO FEELINGS: Stage fave. A good example of how Steve Jones's guitar playing has improved (Compare this with the same track on the Spunk bootleg). Early sneering negative/vacant Pistols lyrics—"You'd better believe I'm in love with myself."

LIAR: Can't play, huh? Stop-start beat with Rotten alternating between rampant wail and sardonic sneer.

GOD SAVE THE QUEEN: The reason three major store chains won't stock the album and are losing large sums of money in potential sales as a result. Hee Hee. This is one of the best singles of all time. Still bursts out of the grooves in all its raging majesty.

PROBLEMS: One of the best tracks and the point where if you ain't done it already you fall off the chair helpless with delight and scream. It must be that killer-riff chord-chugging it locks into near the end. Lashes out at apathy and complacency. "The problem is YOU, whatcha gonna do?"

Side two. SEVENTEEN: "I'm a lazy sod." Very old song. The line about not wearing flares seems to have been dropped between this and the bootleg. "On my face Not a trace Of reality" is one of my favorite lines.

ANARCHY IN THE UK: Wheee! And yet another Best Single of All Time. If you don't know it I don't know where ya bin!

SUBMISSION: The ballad of the album (hee hee). About drowning so you get Special Effects and John doing a strangled gurgle. Metronomic chugging rhythm. Another goodun.

PRETTY VACANT: Yes, yes, yes, you know this one from the single too but so what If the singles are on here. Now it's like having a whole Pistols set on record. You don't have to keep getting up the change the single anyway, AND this is a great track anyway.

NEW YORK: Lashes at the New York rock scene myth, lots of Dolls-lyric hints—"I'm looking for a kiss." Solid and bitchy.

EMI: Here it is! I've already gone on about this one but have a lyric; "It's an unlimited supply, And there is no reason why, I tell you it was all a frame, They only did it cos of fame, Who? EMI!" AND "Blind acceptance is a sign, Of stupid fools that stand in line." LET'S FACE IT. THIS ALBUM WOULD BE A MONSTER EVEN IF IT WAS MEDIOCRE, BAD EVEN THEN THE ABOVE LYRICS WOULD BE TRUE. NEVER MIND COS IT'S A STUNNER. EVEN BETTER THAN THE BUILD-UP BUILT-UP. NEVER MIND THE BOLLOCKS HERE'S THE SEX PISTOLS.

SPUNK—Spunk (Blank)

I dunno, I've waited for a Pistols album to play at home for about a year and now I get TWO of the bastards in the same week!

Still, I'm not gonna grumble. I got this already notorious bootleg of demos and sessions done when Glen Matlock was in the band (which means 1976, mostly the latter half) before the "official" album—the right order cos you can't half see the improvement in the group's playing and style between the two. In most cases the "Bollocks" cuts are superior although the bootleg naturally ain't got such a good sound and the versions of "Submission" and "Anarchy" on SPUNK are better, 'specially the latter where John sounds throatier, deranged and homicidal.

You get the same tracks as on the album PLUS "I Wanna Be Me," the B-side of the "Anarchy" single which should have been on the "Bollocks." There's also "Satellite" but no "Bodies" or "Sun," which is a major bummer but inavoidable cos they weren't written then.

Want this album? You might have a job but I got mine in the dynamic Dean Street Harlequin shop.

NME
5 NOVEMBER 1977
BY JULIE BURCHILL

WHAT ARE YOU waiting for? True love, school to end, Third World/civil war, more wars in the Third World, a leader, the commandos to storm the next aeroplane, next week's NME, The Revolution?

THE SEX Pistols album! Hail, hail, rock and roll, deliver them from evil but lead them not into temptation. Keep them quiet/off the street/content.

Hey punk! You wanna elpee-sized "Anarchy" single? You wanna original "Anarchy" in a black bag? You wanna bootleg album? You wanna collect butterflies? Very fulfilling, collecting things . . . very satisfying. Keep you satisfied, make you fat and old, queuing for the rock and roll show.

The Sex Pistols. They could have dreamed up the name and died. The hysterical equation society makes of love / a gun = power / crime shoved down its own throat, rubbed in its own face. See, I'm just as repressed and contaminated as the next guy. And I like The Sex Pistols. Aesthetically, apart from anything else. Three of them are very good-looking. And the sound of the band goes . . . "I don't wanna holiday in the sun / I wanna go in the city / There's a thousand things I wanna say to you . . . " All very Weller, but is this a Jagger I see before me? No, it's the singles, all four of them—"Anarchy In The UK," "God Save the Queen," "Pretty Vacant" and "Holidays in the Sun"—constituting one third (weigh it) of the vinyl. Of course, there are other great songs. This is no first-round knock-out. This is no Clash attending the CBS Convention; no Damned fucking an American girl with a Fender bass; no Stranglers distorting Trotsky and Lenin for their own cunt-hating, bully-boy ends.

No, this is The Sex Pistols. The band which (so I'm told—I wasn't there in the beginning) started it all. Great songs like "Submission," a numb-nostrilled "Venus In Furs"/"Penetration"/"I Wanna Be Your Dog," in form hypnotic, in content writhing. Pain through a dull, passive haze. Is that a whip in your hand or are you abnormal? Submission / Going Down. down, dragging her down / Submission / I can't tell you what I've found. Smack? Geeks? What's the mystery and who grew up on The New York Dolls? Dogs yelp as the drill continues. Most unhealthy and ya like it like that? Well, it grows on you. A bit like a cancer.

Great songs like "No Feelings": "I got no emotion for anybody else / you better understand I'm in love with myself / My self / My beautiful self." Ah, solipsism rules, as Tony Parsons used to say before he got wise. Good dance tune, anyway, while "Problems" says it all: "Bet you thought you had it all worked out / Bet you thought you knew what I was about / Bet you thought you'd solved all your problems / but YOU are the problem."

Whatcha gonna do? Vegetate? Listen to The Sex Pistols album? Great songs gone, ineffectual flicks of the wrist like "New York," which probably has David JoHansen quaking in his heels, and "EMI"—you guessed it, they're bitching. "You're only twenty-nine / You gotta lot to learn." In spite of this inspired opening. "Seventeen" rambles a little and the guitars do go on a bit. "I just speed / That's all I need."

Whaddyathink of it so far. Well, I've saved the best bit for you to linger over. You've already heard two songs the band co-wrote with Sid Vicious (as opposed to Glen Matlock, The True Pop Kid): "E.M.I." and "Holidays in the Sun." Here's the third. It's called "Bodies." She was a girl from Birmingham.

What? Good God. Was I shocked? Did I jump! Is that what they wanted, to shock people? Smart boys. Do they mean it? Is it satire of the most dubious kind? Did John's Catholic schooling leave its mark? I don't know where "Bodies" is coming from and it scares me. It's obviously a gutter view of sex/dirt/blood/reproduction and if the song is an attack on such a mentality it's admirable.

But, as with "Holidays in the Sun," Rotten never allows himself to make a moral judgement and, going by things he's said, he seems refreshingly capable of making them. I wish he would. I wish he would say that East Germany is presently organising itself better than West

Germany—or vice versa, if that's what he believes. I wish The Sex Pistols had said in "Bodies" that women should not be forced to undergo such savagery, especially within a "Welfare" State.

I'm sick of unlimited tolerance and objectivity, because it leads to annihilation. I wish everyone would quit sitting on the fence in the middle of the road. I think "Bodies" will be open to much misinterpretation and that to issue it was grossly irresponsible.

Many of these songs (under new names) also crop up on their bootleg album—plus "Satellite" in which the Pistols give the finger to the provinces, and "Just Me" which has a nonexistent tune and frightening words: "You wanna be me / Didn't I fool you?" The singing is done with much less expertise, Rotten sounding sick to death. It's a much better record.

I don't really know anything about music but The Sex Pistols seem to play as well as anyone I've heard, and I've heard Jimi Hendrix and Pete Townsend records. I never knew what was meant by "guitar hero"—it sounds like the kind of phrase a mental retard might mouth. "Guitar hero"—you mean as in "war hero," that kind of thing?

Why should anyone wish to play more usefully than Steve Jones, or drum more elaborately than Paul Cook, or play better bass than Sid Vicious? What purpose could it serve to outdo them?

So what are The Sex Pistols? For the tabloids a welcome rest from nubiles (sex and violence in their name alone and drugs too, if you count Rotten's speed dalliance); for the dilettantes, a new diversion (Ritz has a monthly punk column); for the promoters, a new product to push; for the parents, a new excuse; for the kids, a new way (in the tradition of the Boy Scouts, the terraces and One-Up-Man-Ship) in which to dissipate their precious energy. Johnny Rotten, Oliver Twist of this generation; "I wanna some MORE, Malcolm!"

Melody Maker
5 November 1977
by Chris Brazier

And the Rotten visage looms ever larger, leering over Babylon. . . . Surbiton shivers, still lounging in its cheap, holiday in other people's misery; rock's brontosauri look over their shoulders for the ambush, not realising the attack's coming from right out in front.

The album everyone is snarfing up has one of the most tackily unattractive covers ever, one of the most crudely aggressive titles ever, and one of the most brilliant and important sets of lethal rock 'n' roll ever trapped on vinyl.

First and least, let's take the packaging. The Autumn 1977 model is clad in yellow and shocking pink, adorned only by the titles in the Pistols' trademarked traditional black-mailer's news-type (Pistol traditions already?).

BOURGEOIS PROPRIETY: It's pretty functional and it don't care one bit. Why? Disdain for the album-form (I heard a rumour they wanted to be a pure singles band)? Scorn for glossy catch-your-eye commercialism?

Maybe, but I reckon after all this time they could have dreamed up something more special—you can be intelligently, creatively unconventional, after all, and even their singles have pic sleeves.

As for the title, which I slammed the other week when I first heard about it. I've changed my mind—my initial reaction came straight out of the bourgeois notion of propriety and snobbish decency that the Pistols are, and everyone else should be, fighting.

The thing that swung me finally in the title's favor was hearing people say, "why did they do it? They don't need that kind of thing now," implying that the Pistols' rebellion has only ever been a pose, a shortcut to Cadillac Mansion and the Hollywood Highs and that now they've made it they can start being nice boys and let us all sink more comfortably into the diarrhoea of our numbing complacency. That implication's thoroughly obnoxious and fully justifies the title.

The Pistols always meant it I saw them for the first time in April last year and then the song that stood out was "New York," which had a brilliant, improvised attack on the preoccupation with the scene across the Great Divide. In all the times I've seen them, I've never been able to make out the words, and I can't suss many even now, but at least I know now that it numbers a jaded left-over from the decadent scene in 1972: "Four years on you still look the same / I think it's about time you changed your brain / You're just a pile of shit, you're coming to this / You boring old faggot, you steal with a kiss."

THE PROBLEM IS YOU: Challenging people to explode out of the apathy and surrender that decadence had inured them to was always why the Pistols were there, why they were needed. To start us searching again, get us to ask questions, propel us into activity and creativity, instead of becoming more "laid-back" and assuming that the Sixties was a golden age that could never be matched.

Rotten points the finger: "The problem is you! What ya gonna do?"—and he's right. "Eat your heart out on a plastic tray/ You don't do what you want and you'll fade away. If it weren't for me you'd be working nine to five."

No one thinks for themselves, everyone locks up their feelings, doesn't bother with self-expression and the world ends up teetering on a psychic cliff-end—"Claustrophobia, there's too much paranoia—There's too many closets/ Oh when will we fall?" Listen, the Pistols aren't always right (the contempt with which Rotten sneers "faggot" sounds dangerous for a start) but at least they kicked the modern world into gear.

And the kicking was done with rock 'n' roll, of burning revolutionary intensity (revolution is cyclic, not new, remember?), which I guess is what I should be talking about.

Eight of the 12 numbers here were stage faves in the halcyon days before they were signed up, and "Anarchy in the UK" is still the best of them. It really should have opened the album, because those cataclysmic opening chords bursting into Rotten's demonic chuckle will always be the conclusive summary of the band's scything omnipotence—certainly no Pistols LP would have been complete without it. You can almost feel the power-surge sweeping away what's gone before, clearing a place for them at the top of the rockpile, smashing them irresistibly into the nation's con-sciousness.

For my first earful of this platter I aimed at chair-bound objectivity and succeeded, until this track—even after the over-exposure of count-less new wave disco-plays, it's still as fresh as ever. One of rock's all-time classic singles, no question.

It weighs in as side two, track two, propelling the record into a mag-nificent five-song climax. "Submission" is next up, and it's my favorite track at the moment. Reminiscent of the early Stooges, it's the only slow number, hypnotic, like a mantric hang-out loosening you up for the final rush.

But I lose myself as much in this sinuous, darkly attractive chord-sequence as in the brimstone break-out elsewhere, Steve Jones's superb guitar sucking me in as befits a song about drowning in the deep sea of a "watery love." And above it Rotten improvises noises like he used to on stage whenever a string bust. To think they almost left it off.

"Pretty Vacant" follows, that exhilarating drag-you-along intro leading into the message that nothing matters, least of all others' "cheap comments" or their view of us as zilchoids, except that "we know what we feel." And the kiss-off comes with Rotten's two most bitingly cynical vocal performances—"New York" and "EMI." The latter is as bitterly acidic as you'd expect (you can almost see the vitriol eating into the faces of the board of directors), largely a vehicle for the vocal tour de force, but it's a typically incisive Steve Jones solo.

Jones is the best musician in the band—Paul Cook's thrashing is as enthusiastically faultless as Sid Vicious's bass is unspectacular, but who notices bedrock rhythm sections unless they give way?

SPEED-FREAK SNEER: The simple but inspired density of Jones's rhythm-work makes him just as indispensable to the Pistols' sound as Rotten, and as he has an acute grasp of the short, sharp solos which best suit songs like "New York" and "Liar."

Only "Seventeen," almost a throwaway with exaggerated vocals and what sounds like a false chord on the word 'sod' is weaker than "Liar," which is nevertheless compulsive listening for Rotten's variation between speed-freak sneer and bored nonchalance.

Along with "No Feelings," it's much rawer than the Pistols usually are on record, much closer to their live sound—I figure these two numbers, at least, must be the work of Bill Price, who gets a co-credit as producer, vying with Chris Thomas's normal excellent clean-edged feel. "No Feelings" has always been one of their best songs, full-throttle excitement generating a tongue-in-cheek hymn to narcissism/aggressive egocentricity.

What does that leave? "Problems," again faster than usual, with constantly active guitar and a beautifully monotonous, parent-baiting, needle-stuck ending, and "Holidays in the Sun," weakest of the four singles because it packs no killer punch (hookless chorus and a complete non-event masquerading as a guitar solo)—it still wins its bout but only on points.

RAILING AND FLAILING: And "Bodies," the newest number, which copped the rekindled artificial fury of the sewer dailies last week because of its naughty words (they obviously can't have listened to Ian Dury's album, can they?).

But if they'd only stop (unlikely) and think (impossible) for a moment, they'd realise that in a song about abortion some of those words aren't gratuitous anyway, they're horrifically, graphically resonant.

This is the first time I've ever been moved, as opposed to uplifted, by a Sex Pistols' song. Rotten howls his way through a piece of relentlessly driving indignance, railing and flailing against both the tragedy of abortion and the inhuman intolerance of those who would see the girl who has it as "an animal," "a bloody disgrace."

Get this: "Dragged on the table in a factory / An illegitimate place to be / In a package in the lavatory/ Died the little baby SCREAMING / Body, a screaming f——— bloody mess . . . Body—I'm not an animal, Mummy." Raw power, only marred by the thoroughly unnecessary absurdity of "Her name was Polly, she lived in a tree."

Okay, so what's your gripe? The singles? Yeah, well I agree it's a rip-off, whether it was the band, McLaren or Virgin who decided to include the last three singles—all Pistols fans will already have them, and, even if they haven't, they're still on catalogue. I don't know how much weight to give that—all I know is that the inclusion of the singles does make this album more a masterwork than it otherwise might have been.

The classic album from the band the Seventies was waiting for. Do you believe it? Or are you still the problem? What ya gonna do?

Rolling Stone
MARCH 1978
BY PAUL NELSON

If it's not clear to you now, it's going to be: the rock wars of the Seventies have begun, and The Sex Pistols, the most incendiary rock & roll band since The Rolling Stones and The Who, have just dropped the Big One on both the socio-political aridity of their native England and most of the music from which they and we were artistically and philosophically formed. While a majority of young Americans are probably going to misunderstand much of the no-survivors, not-even-us stance of the punk-rock/New Wave anarchy in the UK (compared to which the music of The Ramones sounds like it was invented by Walt Disney). None of us can ignore the movement's savage attack on such stars as the neoaristocratic and undeniably wealthy Rod Stewart, Mick Jagger, Elton John, et al. whose current music the Pistols view as a per-

fect example of jet-set corruption and an utter betrayal of the communal faith. It's obviously kill-the-father time in Great Britain, and, if this is nothing new (after all, Jimmy Porters, England's original Angry Young Man, spewed forth not unlike Johnny Rotten as far back as 1956 in John Osborne's *Look Back in Anger*), it certainly cuts much deeper now because conditions are unquestionably worse. And when one's main enemy is an oppressive mood of collective hopelessness, no one learns faster from experience than the would-be murderer of society, I suppose.

In a commercial sense, however, The Sex Pistols will probably destroy no one but themselves, but theirs is a holy or unholy war that isn't really going to be won or lost by statistics, slick guitar playing or smooth studio work. This band still takes rock & roll personally, as a matter of honour and necessity, and they play with an energy and conviction that is positively transcendent in its madness and fever. Their music isn't pretty—indeed, it often sounds like two subway trains crashing together under forty feet of mud, victims screaming—but it has an Ahab-versus-

THE REVIEWS

Moby Dick power that can shake you like no other music today can. It isn't particularly accessible either, but, hard to believe and maybe not true, record sales apparently don't mean much to the Pistols. (They never do when you don't have any.)

It seems to me that instead of exploiting the commercial potential of revolution, The Sex Pistols have chosen to explore its cultural possibilities. As Greil Marcus pointed out, they "have absorbed from reggae and the Rastas the idea of a culture that will make demands on those in power which no government could ever satisfy; a culture that will be exclusive, almost separatist, yet also messianic, apocalyptic and stoic, and that will ignore or smash any contradiction inherent in such a complexity of stances. . . . 'Anarchy in the UK' is, among other things, a white kid's 'War in a Babylon.'"

But before we make The Sex Pistols and their cohorts into fish-and-chips Zapatas, and long before sainthood has set in on Johnny Rotten, we should remember that this band has more on its mind than being a rock & roll centerpiece for enlightened liberal discussion. First of all, they're musicians, not philosophers, so they're probably more interested in making the best possible mythopoeic loud noise than they are in any logical, inverted political scripture. They're also haters, not lovers, a fact that may worry many Americans since the idea of revolution in this country is usually tinged with workers-unite sentimentality and the pie in the sky of some upcoming utopia.

Johnny Rotten is no Martin Luther King or Pete Seeger—he's more like Bunuel or Celine. He looks at it all and sees right through it, himself included. While he's ranting at England ("a fascist regime") and the Queen ("She ain't no human being"), he doesn't exactly spare his own contingent: "We're so pretty, oh so pretty—We're vacant/ . . . and we don't care."

Musically, *Never Mind the Bollocks, Here's The Sex Pistols* is just about the most exciting rock & roll record of the Seventies. It's all speed, not nuance—drums like the My Lai massacre, bass throbbing like a diseased heart, fifty beats past bursting point, guitars wielded by Jack the Ripper—and the songs all hit like amphetamines or the plague, depending on your point of view. Rotten's jabbing, gabbing vocals won't leave you alone. They either race like crazed, badly wounded soldiers through fields of fire so thick you can't tell the blood from the barrage, or they just stand there in front of you, like amputees in a veterans' hospital, asking where you keep the fresh piles of arms and legs.

Johnny Rotten may be confused, but he's got a right to be. He's flipped the love-hate coin so often that now it's flipping him. Overpowered by his own psychic dynamite, he stands in front of the mirror, "in love with myself, my beautiful self," and the result is "No Feelings." You say, "Holidays in the Sun" and he says, "I wanna go to the new Belsen." On "Bodies," he doesn't know whether he's against an abortion ("screaming bloody fucking mess") or whether he is one. Rotten seems to stroll right through the ego and into the id, and then kick the hell out of it. Talk to him about relationships and you get nowhere: "See my face, not a trace, no reality."

That said, no one should be frightened away from this album. "Anarchy in the UK" and especially "God Save the Queen" are near-perfect rock & roll songs, classics in a way The Who's "My Generation" and The Rolling Stones' "Satisfaction" are. And, contrary to popular opinion, the Pistols do have a sense of humour. They're forever throwing out musical quotes, many of them outlandish (the beginning of "Pretty Vacant" echoes The Who's "Baba O'Riley," the chorus on "EMI" is a direct steal from Jonathan Richman's "Roadrunner," and "New York" completely trashes the Dolls' "Looking for a Kiss"), from groups they obviously at least half admire. If Graham Parker can come away from a Sex Pistols concert saying it was just like seeing the Stones in their glorious early days, just how many contradictions are we talking about?

Those who view The Sex Pistols only in eve-of-destruction terms should remember that any theory of destruction as highfalutin as Rotten's also contains the seeds of freedom and even optimism. Anyone who cares enough to hate this much is probably not a nihilist, but—irony of ironies— a moralist and a romantic as well. I believe it when Johnny Rotten screams, "We mean it, man," in conjunction with destruction, but, in a way, his land's-end, "no future" political position is the most desperately poetic of all. We want to destroy everything, he says, and then see what's left. My guess is that he believes something will be.

DISCOGRAPHY

Authorized Releases

Anarchy in the UK b/w I Wanna Be Me (EMI 2566)
God Save the Queen b/w No Feelings (A&M AMS 7284) [withdrawn]
God Save the Queen b/w Did You No Wrong (Virgin VS 181)
Pretty Vacant b/w No Fun (Virgin VS 184)
Holidays in the Sun b/w Satellite (Virgin VS 191)
(I'm Not Your) Steppin' Stone b/w Pistols Propaganda (VS 339)

Never Mind the Bollocks

MK.1 (Virgin V 2086)

Side 1: *Holidays in the Sun / Liar / No Feelings / God Save the Queen / Problems*

Side 2: *Seventeen / Anarchy in the UK / Bodies / Pretty Vacant / New York / EMI*

Copies come with a one-sided single featuring "Submission." Apparently around 10,000 copies of this version were distributed.

Never Mind the Bollocks

MK.2 (Virgin V 2086)

Side 1: *Holidays in the Sun / Bodies / No Feelings / Liar / God Save the Queen / Problems*

Side 2: *Seventeen / Anarchy in the UK / Submission / Pretty Vacant / New York / EMI*

Also available on CD, this is the standard edition of the album. A picture disc version was also available for a short time.

The Great Rock & Roll Swindle

MK.1 (Virgin VD 2510)

Side 1: *God Save the Queen Symphony / Rock Around the Clock / Johnny B. Goode / Roadrunner* / Black Arabs Medley / Watcha Gonna Do About It* / Anarchy in the UK**

Side 2: *Silly Thing / Substitute* / (Don't You Give Me) No Lip* / (I'm Not Your) Steppin' Stone* / Lonely Boy / Something Else*

Side 3: *L'Anarchie pour le UK / Belsen Was a Gas* / Belsen Was a Gas II / No One Is Innocent / My Way*

Side 4: *C'mon Everybody / EMI (orch.) / The Great Rock & Roll Swindle / You Need Hands / Friggin' in the Riggin*

Again, around 10,000 copies of this version were distributed. Only tracks asterisked feature The Sex Pistols. Strangely enough, there is a CD version available of this Mk.1 version. Indeed, it seems to have now become the stock edition available.

The Great Rock & Roll Swindle

MK.2 (Virgin VD 2510)

Side 1: *God Save the Queen Symphony / Johnny B. Goode / Roadrunner* / Black Arabs Medley / Anarchy in the UK**

Side 2: *Substitute* / (Don't You Give Me) No Lip* / (I'm Not Your) Steppin' Stone* / L'Anarchie pour le UK / Belsen Was a Gas* / Belsen Was a Gas II*

Side 3: *Silly Thing / My Way / I Wanna Be Me* / Something Else / Rock Around the Clock / Lonely Boy / No One Is Innocent*

Side 4: *C'mon Everybody / EMI (orch.) / The Great Rock & Roll Swindle / Friggin' in the Riggin' / You Need Hands / Who Killed Bambi?*

Also available on CD, though the original CD edition, released in the mid-1980s, omitted three tracks. A second, complete edition was subsequently issued.

Kiss This

(Virgin CDV 2702)

CD 1: *Anarchy in the UK / God Save the Queen / Pretty Vacant / Holidays in the Sun / I Wanna Be Me / Did You No Wrong / No Fun / Satellite / (Don't You Give Me) No Lip / (I'm Not Your) Steppin' Stone / Bodies / No Feelings / Liar / Problems / Seventeen / Submission / New York / EMI / My Way / Silly Thing*

Also originally released on vinyl. The first edition came with a "bonus" 9-track CD of the Pistols live in Trondheim, July 21, 1977 (see below).

This Is Crap (Never Mind the Bollocks/Spunk)

(Virgin *Spunk* 1)

CD 1: {*Never Mind the Bollocks* MK.2}

CD 2: *Seventeen / Satellite / No Feelings / I Wanna Be Me / Submission / Anarchy in the UK / God Save the Queen / Problems / Pretty Vacant / Liar / EMI / New York / Problems II / No Feelings II / Pretty Vacant II / Submission II / No Feelings III / EMI II / Satellite II / Seventeen II / Anarchy in the UK*

The lack of annotation on this twofer set a new standard. On CD 2, tracks 1–12 are as per the *Spunk* album, tracks 13–15 are the Spedding demos, tracks 16–20 are the *Bollocks* alternates, and track 21 is the July 1976 demo.

Live in Trondheim July 21, 1977

(Virgin CDVX 2702)

CD1: *Anarchy in the UK / I Wanna Be Me / Seventeen / New York / EMI / No Fun / No Feelings / Problems / God Save the Queen*

The "bonus" CD that came with the first pressing of the *Kiss This* compilation, this is taken from the video that was shot of this show and so it sounds a little ropey for a board tape. But it is a good representation of the band when Vicious was still a functioning member.

Spunk

(Blank 1)

Side 1: *Seventeen / Satellite / No Feelings / I Wanna Be Me / Submission / Anarchy in the UK*

Side 2: *God Save the Queen / Problems / Pretty Vacant / Liar / EMI / New York*

The original 12-track album, compiled from the July 1976 and January 1977 Goodman tapes plus, at the end of side one, the original Wessex "Anarchy in the UK."

No Future UK

Side 1: *Pretty Vacant / Seventeen / Satellite / No Feelings / I Wanna Be Me / Submission / Anarchy in the UK I / Anarchy in the UK II*

Side 2: *No Fun / God Save the Queen / Problems / Pretty Vacant / Liar / EMI / New York*

The original *Spunk* plus the Wessex "No Fun" and the July 1976 versions of "Pretty Vacant" and "Anarchy in the UK." Though originally issued as a bootleg, this was "officially" released on CD and LP in 1989 on Receiver Records. However, the Receiver version is simply taken from a vinyl copy of the bootleg and is best avoided (though it remains the only place the complete "No Fun" is available).

The Mini Album

MK.1 (Mini 1)

Side 1: *Submission / Seventeen / Satellite*

Side 2: *I Wanna Be Me / Anarchy in the UK / No Feelings*

Six of the seven July 1976 demos. Also issued on CD in 1988.

The Mini Album

(Picture Disc) (Antler 37)

Side 1: *Pretty Vacant / Anarchy in the UK / No Feelings*

Side 2: *Submission / Seventeen / Satellite*

"Pretty Vacant" replaces "I Wanna Be Me," pretty damn cheeky, but typical of Lee Woods, the man responsible for *The Mini Album* series.

The Mini Album

MK.2 (Dojo CD 265)

CD1: *Submission / Seventeen / Satellite / I Wanna Be Me / Anarchy in the UK / No Feelings / Pretty Vacant*

At last! A recent CD reissue finally puts all seven Denmark Street demos on a single CD. However, buyers beware: this is the notorious "psychedelic" mix and is therefore something of an acquired taste.

Early Daze

(The Studio Collection) (Dojo CD 119)

CD 1: *I Wanna Be Me / No Feelings / Anarchy in the UK / Satellite / Seventeen / Submission / Pretty Vacant / God Save the Queen / Liar / EMI / New York / Problems*

The best-sounding CD version of the *Spunk* material, though *The Mini Album* probably edges it on the July 1976 demos. Certainly superior to the *Spunk* material on *This Is Crap.*

Pirates of Destiny

(Dojo CD 222)

CD 1: *No Feelings / Seventeen (live) / Problems / Pretty Vacant / I Wanna Be Me (live) / Substitute / (Don't You Give Me) No Lip / (I'm Not Your) Steppin' Stone / Johnny B. Goode / Roadrunner / Watcha Gonna Do About It / Through My Eyes / Seventeen (live)*

Contains two Spedding demos (from a cassette), the original 4-track backing track of the July 1976 "Pretty Vacant," and, most importantly, the original, pre-Jones overdubs, tape of the October 1976 Wessex "covers" session. Many tracks are interspersed with snippets of interviews and adverts.

Wanted—The Goodman Tapes

(Dojo CD 216)

CD 1: *Malcolm McLaren Interview / Satellite / Here We Go Again* / (Don't You Give Me) No Lip (live) / No Fun (live) / Pretty Vacant / Revolution in the Classroom (live) / God Save the Queen (live) / Bill Grundy Interview / EMI / Anarchy in the UK / Submission*

Contains three tracks—"Satellite," "Pretty Vacant," and "Submission"—that purport to be the "original" 4-track versions from July 1976, before new vocals and guitar overdubs were recorded at Riverside

Studios. "Submission" even has some tape spool noises, presumably to add a note of authenticity.

<table>
<tr><td>Live DCs</td><td>

Savage Young Pistols

(Raw Power RP76)

CD 1: *Did You No Wrong / (Don't You Give Me) No Lip / Seventeen / New York / Watcha Gonna Do About It / (I'm Not Your) Steppin' Stone / Submission / Satellite / No Feelings / Pretty Vacant / No Fun / Substitute / Problems / Understanding* + bonus tracks: *Problems / No Feelings / Pretty Vacant / Anarchy in the UK / I Wanna Be Me / Liar / No Feelings*

Curious that the bootlegger should have selected the poorer quality of the two Nashville tapes (April 3, 1976), but a good document of the early Pistols. Bonus tracks are from the second Nashville show (April 23, 1976), the October 1976 Bogarts show, and the (now redundant) Spedding demos.

Agression Thru Repression

(Silver Rarities SIRA 38)

CD 1: *Did You No Wrong / (Don't You Give Me) No Lip / Seventeen / (I'm Not Your) Steppin' Stone / New York / Watcha Gonna Do About It / Submission / Satellite / No Feelings / No Fun / Substitute / Pretty Vacant / Problems* + bonus tracks: *Anarchy in the UK / God Save the Queen / Flowers of Romance / I Wanna Be Me / Liar*

A crude but enjoyable document of one of the most important gigs in the history of rock music: the Pistols' first Manchester gig, at the Lesser Free Trade Hall June 4, 1976. The second encore, "No Fun," is missing but otherwise pure audio verite. Bonus tracks are excellent as well: the "So It Goes," "Anarchy in the UK," the Thorne demo of "No Future," the 100 Club debuts of "Flowers" and "I Wanna Be Me," and the London debut of "Liar" (Screen on the Green, August 29, 1976).

Truly Indecent Exposure

(Colosseum 96-C-004)

CD1: *Anarchy in the UK / I Wanna Be Me / Seventeen / New York / (Don't You Give Me) No Lip / (I'm Not Your) Steppin' Stone / Satellite /*

</td></tr>
</table>

Submission / Liar / Substitute / No Feelings / No Fun / Pretty Vacant / Problems

The definitive version of the 76 Club, Burton-on-Trent, September 24, 1976, tape originally issued on bootleg vinyl as *Indecent Exposure* (but minus "Satellite"). A Goodmanized version of the tape, with three songs missing and the entire running order fucked up (to use the technical term) was issued, somewhat ironically, by EMI's Fame label as *The Original Pistols Live.* It should be avoided at all costs. Stick to the bootlegs, either this Japanese CD or the original vinyl, both taken from the master tape.

Kill the Hippies

(Big 046)

CD 1: *God Save the Queen / I Wanna Be Me / Seventeen / New York / Bodies / Submission / Holidays in the Sun / EMI / No Feelings / Problems / Pretty Vacant / Anarchy in the UK / No Fun / Liar*

The opening show of the U.S. tour, at the Great Southeast Music Hall in Atlanta, in good quality, allegedly a radio broadcast.

Welcome to the Rodeo

(SSR78)

CD 1: *Radio Ad / God Save the Queen / I Wanna Be Me / Seventeen / New York / EMI / Bodies / Belsen Was a Gas / Holidays in the Sun / No Feelings / Problems / Pretty Vacant / Anarchy in the USA / No Fun +* bonus tracks: *Submission / Liar / Anarchy in the UK*

The complete tape of the best of the U.S. shows. Though musically it is still a long way down from the 1976 era, this performance at the Longhorn Ballroom, Dallas, January 10, 1978, has the right balance of audience/artist hostility, Sid's clowning, and Rotten's retorts to get a flavor of what the shows were like. Bonus tracks from Atlanta and Winterland complete the Pistols' January 1978 set.

Thanks to Ted Wood, Mick Marshall, Dave Goodman, Chris Spedding, and Chris Thomas for their input.

GENERAL INDEX

A

"Anarchy in the UK" tour, 53, 55, 59, 63, 129, 134
A&M, 130
    failure of deal with Sex Pistols, 72, 77
    and signing the Sex Pistols, 63, 64–65, 70

B

Bangs, Lester, 102
Barclay Records, 72, 99
The Beatles, 2, 3, 28, 31, 43, 44, 134
Blue Oyster Cult, 90
Bradley, Shanne, 123
Branson, Richard, 72, 78, 93, 94, 98, 111
    fighting ban on NBTB, 113
Bromley Contingent, 5, 10, 63
Buzzcocks, 1, 27, 30

C

Cale, John, 75, 135
CBGBs, 19
The Clash, 27, 30, 43, 53, 78, 87, 88, 118, 142
Cook, Paul, 2, 8, 1, 23, 55, 72, 73, 88, 117, 121, 135, 144
    as drummer, 60, 62, 87, 94, 147
    as lyricist, 11
    reaction to Sid Vicious as new bassist, 64

D

Daltrey, Roger, 64
The Damned, 19, 27, 50, 53, 142
Doll by Doll, 108
The Doors, 26, 123, 124

E

Eddie & the Hot Rods, 5, 8
1889 Indecent Advertisements Act, 112
Emerson, Lake and Palmer, 7
EMI, 2, 18, 23, 31, 33, 49, 50, 54, 56, 128
    concern over Sex pistols, 35, 39, 42, 48
    conservatism of, 54
    dismissal of Pistols, 57, 59, 130
    and legal action against Virgin, 41
    rejection of Goodman's version of "Anarchy in the UK," 41
England's Dreaming (Savage), 19, 77, 99
Eno, Brian, 14

F

The Flowers of Romance, 64, 116, 132
Free Trade hall, 19

G

Goodman, Dave, 2, 3, 59, 61
    and capturing live sound of SP in the studio, 37, 38
    and recording SP, 14–16, 21, 23, 25–27, 33, 47, 60, 99–100, 101, 126
    and recording SP for EMI, 33–34
Gooseberry Studios, 59, 72
Green, Derek, 63
    regretting signing the Sex Pistols, 70

H

The Heartbreakers, 53, 134
Hell, Richard, 122, 123
Hendrix, Jimi, 144
Hynde, Chrissie, 10

I

Independent Broadcasting Authority (IBA), 111
Ingham, John, 9, 17, 18, 51
The Inside Story (Star), 36

J

Jagger, Mick, 109, 148
The Jam, 43
Johansen, David, 62, 143
John, Elton, 148
Jones, Davey, 134
Jones, Steve, 2, 12, 13, 23, 55, 72–73, 117, 119, 126, 128, 135, 144
    as bassist, 66–67, 73, 81, 88, 93
    as guitarist, 26, 27, 3, 42, 48, 60, 62, 87, 88, 106, 140, 146, 147
    and "new wall of sound," 73, 88
    and overdubbing on NMTB, 74, 75, 77, 78
    reaction to Sid Vicious as new bassist, 64
    on SP, 16
Joy Division, 18, 108

K

The Kinks, 106, 123

L

Landsdowne Studios, 34, 72
Levine, Keith, 131
Look Back in Anger (Osborne), 149

M

Magazine, 108
Majestic Studios, 1, 13, 16, 18, 21, 72
Marcus, Greil, 150
The Marquee, 5, 8
Martin, George, 49
Matlock, Glen, 1, 4, 12, 13, 16, 18, 26, 55, 93, 99, 121, 141, 143
    as bassist, 62
    as composer, 27–28, 42, 122–23, 128
    critical of Goodman's production on NBTB, 35
    departure of, as demise of SP, 64, 108
    leaving the SP, 56, 63

    musicianship of, 64
    and return to SP as session musician, 64, 66
McLaren, Malcolm, 2, 8, 9, 10, 12, 107, 148
    arrest for "riverboat gig," 83
    aspirations for SP, 17, 21
    attitudes toward Virgin, 99
    frugality of, 24, 55
    and hiring Johnny Rotten, 12
    influence of, on SP, 33
    and NMTB, 72, 98–100
    and possible role behind bootlegs, 101, 103
    and releasing four singles from NMTB, 95
    response to SP's dismissal from EMI, 57, 59
    role in demise of SP, 64, 117
    and Sex (boutique), 9
    soliciting record companies, 78
    and Chris Thomas, 44–45
Mobbs, Nick, 31, 33
The Monkees, 134
Morrison, Sterling, 7

N

The Nashville, 5, 7, 8, 9, 18, 137
    Sex Pistols banned from, 5
New York Dolls, 12, 44, 122, 123, 141, 151
New York punk scene, 5, 124, 141
Nightingale, Wally, 11, 121
Nirvana, 6

O

Oasis, 6
100 Club, 8, 10, 11, 18, 19, 30, 88, 127
101ers, 8
The Only Ones, 108

P

Parker, Graham, 151
Peel, John, 50
Pink Floyd, 2, 7, 44, 74
Polydor, 71
Presley, Elvis, 73, 128
Price, Bill, 2, 3, 72, 73, 94, 102, 135, 147
    role in producing NMTB, 77, 83, 88, 126

Public Image Limited, 50, 93, 108, 120, 131

R ————————————————

The Ramones, 49, 50, 106, 107, 119, 124, 148
The Rich Kids, 2, 120
Richman, Jonathan, 151
Riverside Studios, 24, 72
The Rolling Stones, 38, 109, 151
Rotten, John, 8, 10, 13, 72, 80–81, 108, 111
    appearance of, 11–12
    contempt for Glen Matlock, 66
    cynicism of, 64, 88, 147
    as frontman, 17
    as lyricist, 11, 19, 42, 43, 92, 96, 121, 123, 126, 128, 129, 130, 140
    rage of, 24, 68, 88
    on Chris Thomas, 73
    on Sid Vicious, 66, 93
    as vocalist, 24, 49–50, 62, 77, 88, 90–91, 94, 95, 103, 135, 142, 143, 148, 150
Rough Trade, 101
Roxy Music, 2, 44, 51, 75, 95
    influence on SP, 72

S ————————————————

Screen on the Green, 30, 31, 45
Sex (boutique), 9, 10
Sex Pistols
    appearance on English TV, 28–30
    banning of, 83
    at Chelmsford Security Prison, 30
    critical response to, 6, 71, 96–97
    criticism of, 18
    final performance of, 117
    image of, 80–82, 85
    impact in America, 107–8
    influence of, 18, 71
    and musical chaos, 89, 93
    musicality of, 6, 7, 9, 15, 16, 64, 88, 127, 130, 149, 150
    notoriety of, 9, 68, 78–79
    at 100 Club, 30
    and "riverboat gig," 82–83
    sense of violence, 16, 17
    at 76 Club, 30
    and signing to EMI, 31, 33, 55
    and signing to Virgin, 61, 71
    sound of, 2, 16, 23, 47, 61, 84, 86, 94, 139, 147
    and touring, 27, 53, 85
    U.S. tour, 54
Sex Pistols Day by Day (Wood), 41
The Shadows, 17
Siouxsie & the Banshees, 108
Small Faces, 9, 26, 106, 132, 133
Smith, Patti, 9, 18, 124
"So It Goes," 29
Spector, Phil, 3, 72
Spedding, Chris, 2, 5, 9, 10, 11, 13, 18, 26
    and recording SP, 14–15, 16, 17, 23, 126
Springsteen, Bruce, 120
Stewart, Rod, 148
The Stooges, 7, 38, 89, 107, 147
The Stranglers, 142
Strummer, Joe, 8

T ————————————————

Television, 5, 64
Thomas, Chris, 2, 3, 42, 43, 51, 61, 71, 94, 96, 102, 128, 135, 147
    and joining the SP, 44, 47, 48
    and NMTB, 73, 74–75, 77, 83, 88, 92
    production methods of, 49, 74–75
    and recording Sid Vicious, 64
Thorne, Mike, 31, 39, 41, 54, 126, 129
"Top of the Pops," 84, 85
Townshend, Pete, 64, 94, 133, 144

V ————————————————

Velvet Underground, 6, 25, 127, 135
Vicious, Sid, 2, 80, 135, 143, 144
    and alcohol abuse, 93
    and "Belsen Was a Gas," 116
    contributions to NMTB, 108
    death of, 120
    incompetence as bassist, 2, 64, 67, 93, 106, 147
    joining SP, 63
    sick with hepatitis, 78
    stupidity of, 64, 93, 103, 132
    violent nature of, 127

Virgin, 4, 61, 71, 75, 94, 97, 98–99, 111, 113, 148
    and advertising "God Save the Queen," 112
    signing SP, 61, 71
    SP's reluctance to sign to, 75

Westwood, Vivienne, 9, 10
The Who, 20, 26, 47, 49, 56, 64, 106, 133, 151
Wilson, Tony, 29
Winterland Ballroom, 117, 120, 132
Wire, 108

W

Wessex Studios, 34, 47, 49, 59, 64, 67, 72, 73, 87

Y

Yes, 7

SONG AND ALBUM INDEX

A

Abbey Road (The Beatles), 43
Aggression thru Repression, 41
"All Day and All of the Night" (Kinks), 26
"All or Nothing" (Small Faces), 132
"Anarchy in the UK" (Sex Pistols), 1, 2, 12,
    23, 24, 29, 31, 81, 89, 90, 94, 116,
    138, 141, 142, 146. 150, 151
      criticism of, 118
Goodman's version of, 38–39, 41, 47,
    48–49, 50, 61, 100, 103, 123, 127–28,
    129
        recording of, 35
        as a single, 33
        sound of, 87
        Thomas's version of, 48, 50, 61,
          73, 88
        vocals on, 24, 29

B

"Baba O'Riley" (The Who), 151
"Belsen Was a Gas" (Sex Pistols), 116,
    117, 130, 138
      notoriety of, 116, 132
Blank Generation (Hell), 122
"Blank Generation" (Hell), 67
Blonde on Blonde (Dylan), 6
Blood on the Tracks (Dylan), 118
"Blue Suede Shoes" (Perkins), 67
"Bodies" (Sex Pistols), 1, 92, 94, 96, 108,
    109, 130, 140, 142, 143, 151
      criticism of, 109
      notoriety of, 114
      point of view in, 92, 131

C

"A Child Is Born" (Mathis), 7
"Complete Control"/"White Man in
    Hammersmith Palais" (The Clash), 67

Concrete Bulletproof Invisible, 35
"The Crying Game" (Berry), 135

D

"Dancing in the Street," 84
"Dancing Queen" (ABBA), 7
Dark Side of the Moon (Pink Floyd), 44, 75
"A Day without Love," 137
"December 1963 (Oh, What a Night)"
    (Four Seasons), 7
"Did You No Wrong" (Sex Pistols), 4, 8, 11,
    12, 24, 77, 78, 96, 121–22

E

"EMI" (Sex Pistols), 56, 60, 62, 67, 77, 88,
    95, 130–31, 138, 139, 141, 143
      criticism of, 91
"The End" (The Beatles), 117

F

"Fernando" (ABBA), 7
First Issue (PiL), 120
"Flowers of Romance" (Sex Pistols), 12,
    19, 126–27, 138
For Your Pleasure (Roxy Music), 44
"Forever and Ever" (Silk), 7
"48 Hours," 85

G

"God Save the Queen" (Sex Pistols), 2, 42,
    60, 62, 67, 74, 77, 96, 116, 129, 138,
    140, 142, 151
      A&M version, 26
      advertisements for, 79, 97
      banning of, 79
      criticism of, 118
      Jones's guitar on, 60
      notoriety of, 109
      Rotten's vocals on, 60

"God Save the Queen" (Sex Pistols)(*cont.*)
    as a single, 87
    as statement, 70
    Sid Vicious learning, 64
    as Virgin single, 78
Great Rock & Roll Swindle (Sex Pistols), 1,
    36, 38, 117, 120, 133, 134, 135, 137
"Guess I'm Falling in Love with Myself
    Again" (Sparks), 26, 126

H ————————————————

"Happiness Is a Warm Gun" (The Beatles),
    43
"Heart of Darkness" (Pere Ubu), 18
Here Come the Warm Jets (Eno), 14
"Hey Girl" (Small Faces), 132
"Holidays in the Sun" (Sex Pistols), 81–83,
    88, 93, 116, 117, 130–31, 140, 142,
    143, 147, 151
        banning of, 109, 116
        criticism of, 90, 96–97, 107, 118
        as a single, 83, 95, 97

I ————————————————

"I Can't Explain"/"Anyway, Anyhow,
    Anywhere" (The Who), 67
"I'm a Believer" (The Monkees), 134
"I'm a Boy" (The Who), 137
"I'm Not Like Everybody Else," 137
"I'm So Bored" (The Clash), 88
"In the City" (The Jam), 96, 130, 140
"Indecent Exposure" (Sex Pistols), 31, 135
"It's My Life," 67
"I Wanna Be Me" (Sex Pistols), 2, 12, 19,
    24, 49, 61, 127, 133, 138, 142
        as B–side to "Anarchy in the UK,"
        25, 62
"I Wanna Be Your Dog" (The Stooges), 143

J ————————————————

"Johnny B. Goode" (Berry), 136, 137
"Jumping Jack Flash"/"Honky Tonk
    Woman" (The Rolling Stones), 67

K ————————————————

Kimono My House (Sparks), 26
Kiss This, 4, 77

L ————————————————

The Lamb Lies Down on Broadway
    (Genesis), 7

Let It Be (The Beatles), 3, 43
"Liar" (Sex Pistols), 43, 60, 62, 77, 128–29,
    138, 140
        criticism of, 90, 128
"Like a Rolling Stone" (Dylan), 134
"Little Johnny Jewel" (Television), 18
"London Boys" (Thunders), 124
"Looking for a Kiss" (New York Dolls),
    151

M ————————————————

"Mamma Mia," 6–7
"Motorbiking" (Spedding), 9
"My Generation" (The Who), 67, 84, 151
"My Mind's Eye" (Small Faces), 132

N ————————————————

*Never Mind the Bollocks, Here's the Sex
    Pistols,* 1–4, 11, 26, 60, 67, 72, 93,
    102, 105, 117, 142
        censorship of, 109, 111, 112–16
        criticism of, 78, 88–89, 89–90,
          105, 106, 118
        delays during recording, 74
        French version of, 98–99
        legal action over, 111, 112
        recording of, 73–74, 77, 102
        release of, 87, 93–94, 95, 98–99,
          111–12
        sound of, 83, 93, 106
"New York" (Sex Pistols), 8, 12, 24, 60, 62,
    72, 77, 124, 138, 141, 143, 151
        criticism of, 90
"No Feelings" (Sex Pistols), 2, 8, 12, 16,
    41, 61, 95, 126, 132, 138, 140, 143,
    151
        as anthem to punk generation, 25
        as B-side of "God Save the
          Queen," 26
        criticism of, 89
        possible source of, 26
"No Fun" (Sex Pistols; orig. The Stooges),
    2, 8, 24, 29, 31, 37, 62, 89, 100, 123,
    133, 135
        as B-side to "Pretty Vacant," 38
"No Future" (Sex Pistols), 41, 60, 61,
    62
        Goodman's version, 63
        Thomas's version, 63
No Future UK (Sex Pistols), 38, 100
"No Lip" (Berry), 8, 37, 134–35

P

Paris 1919 (Cale), 44
"Penetration," 143
Pirates of Destiny, 4, 36, 134, 137
"Piss Factory" (Smith), 18
"Play with Fire" (Rolling Stones), 134
"Pretty Vacant" (Sex Pistols), 2, 8, 11–14,
   16, 25, 29, 49, 60, 74, 87, 96, 97, 100,
   122–23, 129, 135, 138, 141, 151
      criticism of, 48
      as EMI's choice for first single, 33
      as single, 83–84, 85
      sound of, 17
      Chris Thomas on, 47
"Problems" (Sex Pistols), 8, 12, 16, 24, 41,
   60, 62, 76, 89, 95, 98, 126, 132, 138,
   141, 143
"Psychotic Reaction," 137

R

"Raw Power" (The Stooges), 84
"Remote Control" (The Clash), 78
"Roadrunner" (Richman), 136, 151

S

"Satellite" (Sex Pistols), 4, 12, 25, 62, 77,
   90, 95, 98, 124–25, 142
      criticism of, 91
"(I Can't Get No) Satisfaction" (Rolling
   Stones), 67, 84, 151
Saturn Strip (Vega), 118
*Sergeant Pepper's Lonely Hearts Club
   Band* (The Beatles), 6, 91, 119
"Seventeen" (Sex Pistols), 8, 11, 12, 77,
   88, 95, 122, 141, 143
"Sha La La La Lee" (Small Faces), 132
"SOS" (ABBA), 123

"Stupidity" (Dr. Feelgood), 16
"(Smells Like) Teen Spirit" (Nirvana), 118
Spunk (Sex Pistols), 3, 4, 23, 60, 99–100,
   101, 102–3, 106
"Steppin' Stone" (Sex Pistols; orig. The
   Monkees), 8, 37, 89, 132, 134, 135
The Stooges, 135
"Submission" (Sex Pistols), 8, 11, 12, 24,
   25, 61, 62, 94–96, 97–98, 99, 102,
   106, 123–24, 141, 143, 146
      alternate version, 93
      criticism of, 89, 90, 107
"Substitute" (Sex Pistols; orig. The Who), 8,
   37, 89, 133–34

T

This Is Crap (Sex Pistols), 16, 26, 67, 77

U

"Understanding" (Small Faces), 132

V

"Venus in Furs" (Velvet Underground),
   143

W

Wanted: The Goodman Tapes (Sex Pistols),
   4, 25
"Wham Bam, Thank You Ma'am" (Small
   Faces), 123
"Whatcha Gonna Do About It, 36, 37,
   132–33, 135
The White Album (The Beatles), 43
White Light/White Heat (Velvet Under-
   ground), 25
"White Riot" (The Clash), 71
Wish You Were Here (Pink Floyd), 7